❖❖

Getting Disputes Resolved

William L. Ury
Jeanne M. Brett
Stephen B. Goldberg

Getting Disputes Resolved

Designing Systems to
Cut the Costs of Conflict

Jossey-Bass Publishers

San Francisco   •   London   •   1988

GETTING DISPUTES RESOLVED
Designing Systems to Cut the Costs of Conflict
by William L. Ury, Jeanne M. Brett, and Stephen B. Goldberg

Copyright © 1988 by: Jossey-Bass Inc., Publishers
350 Sansome Street
San Francisco, California 94104
&
Jossey-Bass Limited
28 Banner Street
London EC1Y 8QE

Library of Congress Cataloging-in-Publication Data

Ury, William.
Getting disputes resolved.

(A Joint publication in the Jossey-Bass management
series and the Jossey-Bass social and behavioral science
series)
Bibliography: p.
Includes index.
1. Conflict management. I. Brett, Jeanne M.
II. Goldberg, Stephen B. III. Title. IV. Series:
Jossey-Bass management series. V. Series: Jossey-Bass
social and behavioral science series.
HD42.U79 1988   658.4   88-42805
ISBN 1-55542-125-3 (alk. paper)

Manufactured in the United States of America

The paper in this book meets the guidelines for
permanence and durability of the Committee on
Production Guidelines for Book Longevity of the
Council on Library Resources.

JACKET DESIGN BY WILLI BAUM

FIRST EDITION

Code 8855

❖❖

A joint publication in
The Jossey-Bass Management Series
and
The Jossey-Bass Social and
Behavioral Science Series

To Valerie, Gillian, Amanda, and Benjamin,
dispute systems designers of the future

Contents

Preface

How can you persuade people or organizations to talk more and fight less? If they regularly deal with their problems by going to court, striking, threatening to break off the relationship, or physically attacking each other, how can you encourage them to negotiate their differences instead? If the relationship or organization is new—a marriage, a corporate joint venture, or a company—how can you help ensure that future disputes are handled effectively and cooperatively?

You may be a manager faced with an ongoing series of disputes with or among employees, with customers or vendors, or with other departments. You may be a lawyer wondering how to draw up a partnership contract to ensure that disputes will be negotiated not litigated. Or you may be a dispute resolution professional—a mediator, court administrator, or family counselor—working with people who are continually doing battle at high cost to themselves and to the community. You may be involved in the disputes yourself or you may be an outsider.

Whatever your situation, the costs of disputing—lawyers' fees, lost wages and production, physical and emotional injuries—are often too high. In addition, the outcomes of disputes are generally unsatisfying: people do not get what they want or need, relationships are strained, agreements collapse, old disputes reemerge. The consequences of such disputing patterns may be severe: in a business, lowered productivity and profitability;[1] in a marriage, unhappy children and divorce; among nations, bloodshed and war.

While some disputes can be prevented, many cannot. Disputes are inevitable when people with different interests deal with each other regularly. Those different interests will come into conflict from time to time, generating disputes. These disputes can have constructive consequences if the parties air their different interests, make difficult trade-offs, reach a settlement that satisfies the essential needs (if not aspirations) of each, and move on to cooperate in other realms. This process can help people and organizations grow and change.

If disputes are inevitable, what can you do to get them resolved satisfactorily? In a particular dispute, you might be able to step in and personally try to settle it. But even if you succeed, the underlying conflict of interests that generated the dispute will remain. New disputes will arise, and the parties may go back to fighting. If you want to have an impact beyond a single dispute, the challenge is to develop procedures that the parties will use, even in your absence, to resolve disputes more satisfactorily and at lower cost.

This was the challenge facing union and management officials at International Harvester in the early 1960s. At that time, few employee grievances were being settled by negotiation, and many were being taken to costly arbitration. Finally, the permanent arbitrator, David Cole, urged union and management officials to work together on new procedures designed to resolve grievances orally on the day they arose. The improvement was dramatic: at one plant, for example, the number of written grievances dropped from 450 to 3 per month. Throughout the entire company, grievances took less time, relations between labor and management improved, and a strike over the terms of a new contract was averted for the first time in twelve years.[2]

A similar challenge faced IBM and Fujitsu in the 1980s. The two computer giants had wrangled for years over hundreds of disputes in which IBM charged that Fujitsu had stolen IBM software. At an impasse, IBM and Fujitsu, with the help of arbitrators Robert Mnookin and John Jones, negotiated a set of procedures allowing Fujitsu to examine and use IBM software in exchange for adequate compensation. The result: future disputes about use are to be resolved by a neutral technical expert; future disputes about compensation are to be resolved by the arbitrators.[3]

A similar challenge arose at Bryant High School in New York. Troubled by tensions and violence, the school instituted a mediation program in the early 1980s. Dozens of students, teachers, administrators, and parents were intensively trained in mediation skills. These new mediators resolved disputes ranging from student-teacher and student-parent problems to student fistfights. The number of suspensions for fighting dropped drastically, and the school's overall climate improved. The successful program was extended to other high schools and has since been used nationwide.[4]

In many families, conflicts between parents and their rebellious teenagers are handled through confrontation and fighting, often ending up in court. Even if the particular problem that brought the family to court is resolved, the underlying conflicts are not, so the cycle of confrontation, fighting, and court continues. In an effort to break this cycle, the Children's Hearings Project in Massachusetts taught families to use negotiation and avoidance to deal with their problems rather than confrontation and fighting. Six to nine months after the hearing, two-thirds of the participating families reported less arguing and fighting, and almost half said they handled conflict by talking things over.[5]

Each of these examples illustrates how changing the procedures for dispute resolution can reduce the costs of disputing. Changing procedures alone, however, is not enough; disputants must have the motivation, skills, and resources to use the new procedures. The challenge is to change the dispute resolution system—the overall set of procedures used and the factors affecting their use—in order to encourage people and organizations to talk instead of fight about their differences.

Designing a dispute resolution system is somewhat like designing a flood control system. Like rainfall, conflict is inevitable. Properly controlled, it can be a boon; too much in the wrong place can create a problem. The challenge is to build a structure that will direct disputes along a low-cost path to resolution. *Getting Disputes Resolved* addresses this challenge.

Aims and Audience

This book is based on our own experiences as designers of dispute resolution systems in the coal industry and the experiences of others who have designed systems for corporations, government offices, schools, churches, neighborhoods, families, and nations. In this book, we attempt to distill the lessons we and others have learned from these experiences and offer a detailed case study of our own efforts in the coal industry.

This book is intended for several audiences. One audience is people who handle disputes as part of their profession: lawyers, mediators, diplomats, judges, arbitrators, union representatives, personnel managers, ombudsmen, court administrators, and family counselors. Another audience is those who, concerned by the costs of conflict in their organizations or relationships, want to design a better dispute resolution system. They may be directors of customer relations seeking to streamline procedures for dealing with customer complaints, CEOs searching for ways to resolve disputes arising in a joint venture, or government officials concerned with endless court challenges to administrative regulations. A similar audience consists of organizational consultants who may be called in to solve another problem, such as low productivity, only to discover that a key part of the solution is changing the dispute resolution system. A fourth audience for this book is scholars, researchers, and students concerned with understanding, developing and evaluating alternative dispute resolution systems.

Overview

We begin this book by presenting the basic conceptual framework underlying our approach. In Chapter One we distinguish three major ways of resolving disputes: to reconcile the disputants' underlying interests, to determine who is right, and to determine who has more power. Problem-solving negotiation exemplifies the interests approach; going to court, the rights approach; strikes and wars, the power approach. We argue that, in general, an interests approach is less costly and more rewarding than a rights approach, which in turn is less costly and more rewarding than a power approach. The goal, then, is to design a system that provides interests-based procedures for disputants to use whenever possible and low-cost rights procedures (such as advisory arbitration) or low-cost power procedures (such as voting) as backups.

The first step in moving toward such a new system is to diagnose the existing system. In Chapter Two we present a model of a dispute resolution system. The diagnosis focuses on three questions: What types of disputes arise? How are they handled? Why do disputants use some procedures and not others? Pinpointing some of the underlying factors—lack of procedures, motivation, skills, and resources—may suggest what changes to make. Can procedures be devised that meet the same needs at a lower cost?

We set forth six basic principles of dispute systems design in Chapter Three. The first is to put the focus on interests. The second is to design procedures that encourage disputants to return to negotiation—procedures we term *loopbacks*. The third is to provide low-cost rights and power procedures that, if all else fails, can bring about a final resolution of a dispute. The fourth is to prevent disputes whenever possible by building in a consultation procedure and a procedure for constructive feedback after a dispute. The fifth is to arrange the different procedures in a sequence from least to more costly. The final principle is to provide the motivation, skills, and resources necessary to make all the procedures work. The application of these six principles results in a low-cost dispute resolution system.

These principles alone, however, will not necessarily produce a workable system. As we demonstrate in Chapter

Four, designing a dispute system is not just a technical task of making the best changes; it is also a political task of garnering support, dealing with resistance, and motivating people to use the changed procedures. Nor is it just a question of having the right answer and then convincing the parties. Often the participants have useful ideas about what is wrong and what is needed, what will and will not work in their situation. The designer's knowledge must be blended with theirs. Furthermore, the design process may require mediating among parties who disagree about what changes are appropriate. Working with the parties—involving them in the process of diagnosis, design, and implementation—is thus a critical element of dispute systems design.

After we explain the process of diagnosing, designing, and implementing changes in the dispute system, we present a detailed case study in dispute systems design in the coal industry. In Chapter Five we describe Brett and Goldberg's 1978 study of wildcat strikes in the bituminous coal industry, which had reached a level of over 3,000 strikes per year. On the basis of that study, they concluded that a coal mine could operate without frequent wildcat strikes but to do so required establishing a problem-solving relationship between mine managers and the union.

Then in 1980, as we relate in Chapter Six, we worked as a team on what was probably the most strike-ridden mine in the coal industry. Caney Creek mine had suffered thirty wildcat strikes in the previous two years—along with bomb threats, layoffs, sabotage, and the overnight jailing of 115 miners.[6] The situation was so costly that the company was seriously considering closing the mine altogether. Working with suggestions from union and management officials, we set about diagnosing the problem and designing a program of changes intended to encourage negotiation between miners and managers. We tried to mediate the adoption of the changes, and then we helped the parties put the program into practice. After our intervention, wildcat strikes at Caney Creek ceased for nearly a year. Grievances were negotiated successfully. The mine's productivity increased significantly, and the laid-off miners returned to their jobs. Eight years later, the improved dispute resolution system remains in use.

In Chapter Seven we describe Goldberg's efforts to take what we had learned about dispute systems design at a single mine and apply it on an industrywide basis. Beginning in 1980 he sought to change the coal industry's system for resolving grievances by introducing interests-based mediation as an alternative to rights-based arbitration. Mediation promised to be faster and less expensive than arbitration and to produce more satisfactory outcomes. This promise was soon fulfilled, but while the mediation procedure has since spread to other industries, it has also met with considerable resistance. This chapter discusses the sources of resistance and Goldberg's efforts to overcome it.

In sum, the book presents a basic conceptual framework for dispute systems design, a variety of lessons and examples for practitioners, and a detailed case study. Dispute systems design is a practical method for cutting the costs of conflict and, at the same time, achieving the gains that come from satisfactory resolutions. The distinctive contribution of a systems approach is that it addresses not just a single dispute but the series of disputes that occur—and will continue to occur—in any relationship or organization.

Lincoln, Massachusetts   William L. Ury
Chicago, Illinois   Jeanne M. Brett
Venasque, France   Stephen B. Goldberg
September 1988

Acknowledgments

In looking back on our three projects in the coal industry, we sensed a coherence, but we did not quite know how to capture it. Like Molière's Monsieur Jourdain, who was astounded one day to discover that all his life he had been speaking "prose," we wanted to know what language we had been speaking. We were not mediators—that is, we were not trying to settle specific disputes. Rather, we were trying to change the way in which the parties handled their disputes.

We decided to write a book on the subject that presented our own experiences as well as those of others who, in contexts ranging from families to corporations and from neighborhoods to nations, had engaged in the same task of what we came to call dispute systems design.

We are indebted to many people and institutions for the assistance they provided. Our horizons were expanded and our perspective enriched by the designers who spent many hours sharing their experiences and wisdom with us: Richard Chasin, John Dunlop, Mary Margaret Golten, Eric Green, William Hobgood, Deborah Kolb, Michael Lewis, Bernard Mayer, Marguerite Millhauser, Robert Mnookin, Christopher Moore, Richard Salem, Carl Schneider, Raymond Shonholtz, Sylvia Skratek, Linda Singer, Karl Slaikeu, Lawrence Susskind, Marty Van Parys, and Susan Wildau. Their work confirmed for us the existence of general design principles that apply across different contexts.

The book benefited immensely from the comments of those who read earlier drafts of the manuscript. The comments challenged us to deal with difficult issues we might otherwise have ignored. Many of the designers we interviewed offered suggestions, as did Graham Allison, James Anderson, Max Bazerman, Phillip Cousins, Harry Edwards, Julius Getman, Thomas Kochan, David Lax, Michael LeRoy, Roy Lewicki, Martin Linsky, Robert McKersie, Jeffrey Rubin, Marc Sarkady, Frank Sander, Mark Sommer, and Rolf Valtin. We are deeply grateful to each of them. In addition, Stephen Bates gave us first-rate editorial assistance.

We profited greatly from the informal feedback we received at seminars conducted at the Program on Negotiation at Harvard Law School, the Dispute Resolution Research Center at Northwestern University, and the Institut d'Administration des Entreprises at the University of Aix-Marseille (France).

We were fortunate to have the careful and competent administrative and secretarial services of Joann Dillon, Melissa Ferrell, Jessy Johnson, Linda Lane, Julie McLaughlin, and Lucia Miller. The accuracy and form of all references were checked by Lisa Bartosic, Beth Cataldo, and John Santa Lucia. Beth Cataldo also coordinated the final copyediting.

Funding for the wildcat strike study (Chapter Five) was provided by the National Science Foundation, and funding for the initial experiment in grievance mediation (Chapter Seven) was provided by the U.S. Department of Labor. Financial assistance in writing the book was provided to Jeanne Brett by the J. L. Kellogg Professorship in Dispute Resolutions and Organizations, to Stephen Goldberg by grants from the Julias Rosenthal Fund and the Kathleen M. Haight Law School Fund for Research, and to all of us by the Dispute Resolution Research Center at Northwestern University under a grant from the William and Flora Hewlett Foundation. William Ury is indebted to the Avoiding Nuclear War Project at the John F. Kennedy School of Government, funded by the

Carnegie Corporation, for generously supporting him while this book was written.

William Hicks, our editor at Jossey-Bass, championed the book, offered valuable editorial advice, and gently and wisely pushed us to finish. Elizabeth Sherwood applied her considerable editorial gifts to improving the manuscript and added her enthusiastic moral support. We are very grateful indeed.

Finally, we want to express our appreciation to the coal miners and managers who participated in the wildcat strike study, worked with us at Caney Creek, and helped establish grievance mediation. Without their stimulation, there would be no book.

❖❖

The Authors

William L. Ury is associate director of the Program on Negotiation at Harvard Law School. He received his B.A. degree (1975) in anthropology and linguistics from Yale University and his M.A. degree (1977) and Ph.D. degree (1982) in social anthropology from Harvard University.

Ury's research has focused on negotiation, mediation, and crisis management. He has served as a mediator, arbitrator, and dispute systems designer and has worked extensively on labor, business, and international conflicts.

From 1982 to 1984, Ury was an assistant professor at Harvard Business School. And from 1983 to 1988, he was associate director of the Avoiding Nuclear War Project at Harvard University's Kennedy School of Government, where he directed a joint study group on crisis prevention with scholars and policy advisors from the United States and the Soviet Union. Ury has been involved in efforts to prevent accidental nuclear war through the creation of nuclear risk reduction centers in Washington, D.C., and Moscow, and he has served as a consultant to the Crisis Management Center at the White House.

Ury's books include *Getting to Yes: Negotiating Agreement Without Giving In* (1981, with R. Fisher) and *Beyond the Hotline: How Crisis Control Can Prevent Nuclear War* (1985).

Jeanne M. Brett is the J. L. Kellogg Professor of Dispute Resolution and Organizations at the Kellogg Graduate School of Management, Northwestern University. She joined the faculty of Northwestern University in 1976, and in 1984 she became the director of the university's Dispute Resolution Research Center.

After receiving her A.M. degree (1969) in industrial relations and her Ph.D. degree (1972) in psychology from the University of Illinois, Brett joined the psychology faculty there. In 1975 she moved to the University of Michigan as assistant professor of psychology.

Brett initiated negotiations training for management students at the Kellogg Graduate School of Management in 1981 and for the school's extensive executive programs in 1982. The negotiation and third-party dispute resolution teaching materials she helped to develop for the National Institute for Dispute Resolution and the American Arbitration Association are currently used in courses at over 100 business schools. In a 1987 alumni survey at the Kellogg Graduate School of Business, the negotiations course Brett developed was the most highly recommended of all the courses offered at the school.

Brett is an active researcher in two areas: dispute resolution and work and family. She is the author or coauthor of two books and over thirty articles.

Stephen B. Goldberg is Professor of Law at Northwestern University Law School. He received his A.B. degree from Harvard University (1954) and his L.L.B. degree (1959) from Harvard Law School. He also spent a year as a graduate student at the London School of Economics.

Goldberg began his academic career at the University of Illinois College of Law in 1965. In 1973 he was appointed visiting scholar at the American Bar Foundation and in 1974 he took up his current position at Northwestern University Law School. His tenure there was temporarily interrupted in 1979–80, when he was visiting professor at Harvard Law School and consultant to President Carter's Commission on Coal.

Goldberg is the coauthor of *Union Representation Elections: Law and Reality* (1976, with J. Herman and J. Getman) and *Dispute Resolution* (1985, with E. Green and F. Sander), which won the 1985 Center for Public Resources book prize for excellence and innovation in alternative dispute resolution. In 1987 the Society of Professionals in Dispute Resolution presented Goldberg with the Willoughby Abner Award for practical research in public service labor-management relations.

◆◇

Getting Disputes Resolved

❖❖

Part One

Understanding and Designing Dispute Resolution Systems

The next four chapters set out a basic framework for dispute systems design. Chapter One presents the goal of design: an interests-based system. Chapter Two suggests how to diagnose what is wrong with the situation as it exists or, if the relationship or organization does not yet exist, what is needed. Chapter Three discusses how to go about designing an improved system. And Chapter Four considers the process of working with the parties to carry out the diagnosis and design and to put the changes into place.

The framework is based on the lessons we have drawn from our experiences as designers as well as those of other designers whom we have interviewed. We recognize that many of the ideas are new and untested, so we offer this framework not as a definitive approach but rather as an initial foray into what we hope will one day become a full-fledged field of theory and practice.

❖❖

Chapter 1

Three Approaches to Resolving Disputes

Interests, Rights, and Power

It started with a pair of stolen boots. Miners usually leave their work clothes in baskets that they hoist to the ceiling of the bathhouse between work shifts. One night a miner discovered that his boots were gone.[1] He couldn't work without boots. Angry, he went to the shift boss and complained: "Goddammit, someone stole my boots! It ain't fair! Why should I lose a shift's pay and the price of a pair of boots because the company can't protect the property?"

"Hard luck!" the shift boss responded. "The company isn't responsible for personal property left on company premises. Read the mine regulations!"

The miner grumbled to himself, "I'll show them! If I can't work this shift, neither will anyone else!" He convinced a few buddies to walk out with him and, in union solidarity, all the others followed.

The superintendent of the mine told us later that he had replaced stolen boots for miners and that the shift boss should have done the same. "If the shift boss had said to the miner, 'I'll buy you a new pair and loan you some meanwhile,' we wouldn't have had a strike." The superintendent believed that his way of resolving the dispute was better than

3

the shift boss's or the miner's. Was he right and, if so, why? In what ways are some dispute resolution procedures better than others?

In this chapter, we discuss three ways to resolve a dispute: reconciling the interests of the parties, determining who is right, and determining who is more powerful. We analyze the costs of disputing in terms of transaction costs, satisfaction with outcomes, effect on the relationship, and recurrence of disputes. We argue that, in general, reconciling interests costs less and yields more satisfactory results than determining who is right, which in turn costs less and satisfies more than determining who is more powerful. The goal of dispute systems design, therefore, is a system in which most disputes are resolved by reconciling interests.

Three Ways to Resolve Disputes

The Boots Dispute Dissected

A dispute begins when one person (or organization) makes a claim or demand on another who rejects it.[2] The claim may arise from a perceived injury or from a need or aspiration.[3] When the miner complained to the shift boss about the stolen boots, he was making a claim that the company should take responsibility and remedy his perceived injury. The shift boss's rejection of the claim turned it into a dispute. To resolve a dispute means to turn opposed positions—the claim and its rejection—into a single outcome.[4] The resolution of the boots dispute might have been a negotiated agreement, an arbitrator's ruling, or a decision by the miner to drop his claim or by the company to grant it.

In a dispute, people have certain interests at stake. Moreover, certain relevant standards or rights exist as guideposts toward a fair outcome. In addition, a certain balance of power exists between the parties. Interests, rights, and power then are three basic elements of any dispute. In resolving a dispute, the parties may choose to focus their attention on one or more of these basic factors. They may seek to (1) reconcile their underlying interests, (2) determine who is right, and/or (3) determine who is more powerful.

When he pressed his claim that the company should do something about his stolen boots, the miner focused on rights—"Why should I lose a shift's pay and the price of a pair of boots because the company can't protect the property?" When the shift boss responded by referring to mine regulations, he followed the miner's lead and continued to focus on who was right. The miner, frustrated in his attempt to win what he saw as justice, provoked a walkout—changing the focus to power. "I'll show them!" In other words, he would show the company how much power he and his fellow coal miners had—how dependent the company was on them for the production of coal.

The mine superintendent thought the focus should have been on interests. The miner had an interest in boots and a shift's pay, and the company had an interest in the miner working his assigned shift. Although rights were involved (there was a question of fairness) and power was involved (the miner had the power to cause a strike), the superintendent's emphasis was on each side's interests. He would have approached the stolen boots situation as a joint problem that the company could help solve.

Reconciling Interests

Interests are needs, desires, concerns, fears—the things one cares about or wants. They underlie people's positions—the tangible items they *say* they want. A husband and wife quarrel about whether to spend money for a new car. The husband's underlying interest may not be the money or the car but the desire to impress his friends; the wife's interest may be transportation. The director of sales for an electronics company gets into a dispute with the director of manufacturing over the number of TV models to produce. The director of sales wants to produce more models. Her interest is in selling TV sets; more models mean more choice for consumers and hence increased sales. The director of manufacturing wants to produce fewer models. His interest is in decreasing manufacturing costs; more models mean higher costs.

Reconciling such interests is not easy. It involves probing for deep-seated concerns, devising creative solutions, and making trade-offs and concessions where interests are opposed.[5] The most common procedure for doing this is *negotiation,* the act of back-and-forth communication intended to reach agreement. (A procedure is a pattern of interactive behavior directed toward resolving a dispute.) Another interests-based procedure is *mediation,* in which a third party assists the disputants in reaching agreement.

By no means do all negotiations (or mediations) focus on reconciling interests. Some negotiations focus on determining who is right, such as when two lawyers argue about whose case has the greater merit. Other negotiations focus on determining who is more powerful, such as when quarreling neighbors or nations exchange threats and counterthreats. Often negotiations involve a mix of all three—some attempts to satisfy interests, some discussion of rights, and some references to relative power. Negotiations that focus primarily on interests we call "interests-based," in contrast to "rights-based" and "power-based" negotiations. Another term for interests-based negotiation is *problem-solving negotiation,* so called because it involves treating a dispute as a mutual problem to be solved by the parties.

Before disputants can effectively begin the process of reconciling interests, they may need to vent their emotions. Rarely are emotions absent from disputes. Emotions often generate disputes, and disputes, in turn, often generate emotions. Frustration underlay the miner's initial outburst to the shift boss; anger at the shift boss's response spurred him to provoke the strike.

Expressing underlying emotions can be instrumental in negotiating a resolution. Particularly in interpersonal disputes, hostility may diminish significantly if the aggrieved party vents her anger, resentment, and frustration in front of the blamed party, and the blamed party acknowledges the validity of such emotions or, going one step further, offers an apology.[6] With hostility reduced, resolving the dispute on the basis of interests becomes easier. Expressions of emotion have a special place in certain kinds of interests-based negotiation and mediation.

Determining Who Is Right

Another way to resolve disputes is to rely on some independent standard with perceived legitimacy or fairness to determine who is right. As a shorthand for such independent standards, we use the term *rights*. Some rights are formalized in law or contract. Other rights are socially accepted standards of behavior, such as reciprocity, precedent, equality, and seniority.[7] In the boots dispute, for example, while the miner had no contractual right to new boots, he felt that standards of fairness called for the company to replace personal property stolen from its premises.

Rights are rarely clear. There are often different—and sometimes contradictory—standards that apply. Reaching agreement on rights, where the outcome will determine who gets what, can often be exceedingly difficult, frequently leading the parties to turn to a third party to determine who is right. The prototypical rights procedure is adjudication, in which disputants present evidence and arguments to a neutral third party who has the power to hand down a binding decision. (In mediation, by contrast, the third party does not have the power to decide the dispute.) Public adjudication is provided by courts and administrative agencies. Private adjudication is provided by arbitrators.[8]

Determining Who Is More Powerful

A third way to resolve a dispute is on the basis of power. We define power, somewhat narrowly, as the ability to coerce someone to do something he would not otherwise do. Exercising power typically means imposing costs on the other side or threatening to do so. In striking, the miners exercised power by imposing economic costs on the company. The exercise of power takes two common forms: acts of aggression, such as sabotage or physical attack, and withholding the benefits that derive from a relationship, as when employees withhold their labor in a strike.

In relationships of mutual dependence, such as between labor and management or within an organization or a family, the question of who is more powerful turns on who is less dependent on the other.[9] If a company needs the employees' work more than employees need the company's pay, the company is more dependent and hence less powerful. How dependent one is turns on how satisfactory the alternatives are for satisfying one's interests. The better the alternative, the less dependent one is. If it is easier for the company to replace striking employees than it is for striking employees to find new jobs, the company is less dependent and thereby more powerful. In addition to strikes, power procedures include behaviors that range from insults and ridicule to beatings and warfare. All have in common the intent to coerce the other side to settle on terms more satisfactory to the wielder of power. Power procedures are of two types: power-based negotiation, typified by an exchange of threats, and power contests, in which the parties take actions to determine who will prevail.

Determining who is the more powerful party without a decisive and potentially destructive power contest is difficult because power is ultimately a matter of perceptions. Despite objective indicators of power, such as financial resources, parties' perceptions of their own and each other's power often do not coincide. Moreover, each side's perception of the other's power may fail to take into account the possibility that the other will invest greater resources in the contest than expected out of fear that a change in the perceived distribution of power will affect the outcomes of future disputes.

Interrelationship Among Interests, Rights, and Power

The relationship among interests, rights, and power can be pictured as a circle within a circle within a circle (as

Figure 1. Interrelationships Among Interests, Rights, and Power.

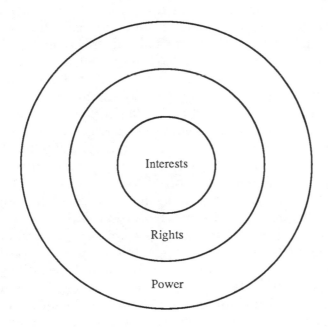

in Figure 1). The innermost circle represents interests; the middle, rights; and the outer, power. The reconciliation of interests takes place within the context of the parties' rights and power. The likely outcome of a dispute if taken to court or to a strike, for instance, helps define the bargaining range within which a resolution can be found. Similarly, the determination of rights takes place within the context of power. One party, for instance, may win a judgment in court, but unless the judgment can be enforced, the dispute will continue. Thus, in the process of resolving a dispute, the focus may shift from interests to rights to power and back again.

Lumping It and Avoidance

Not all disputes end with a resolution. Often one or more parties simply decide to withdraw from the dispute. Withdrawal takes two forms. One party may decide to "lump it," dropping her claim or giving in to the other's claim because she believes pursuing the dispute is not in her interest, or because she concludes she does not have the power to resolve it to her satisfaction. The miner would have been lumping his claim if he had said to himself, "I strongly disagree with management's decision not to reimburse me for my boots, but I'm not going to do anything about it." A second form of withdrawal is avoidance. One party (or both) may decide to withdraw from the relationship, or at least to curtail it significantly.[10] Examples of avoidance include quitting the organization, divorce, leaving the neighborhood, and staying out of the other person's way.

Both avoidance and lumping it may occur in conjunction with particular dispute resolution procedures. Many power contests involve threatening avoidance—such as threatening divorce—or actually engaging in it temporarily to impose costs on the other side—such as in a strike or breaking off of diplomatic relations. Many power contests end with the loser lumping her claim or her objection to the other's claim. Others end with the loser engaging in avoidance: leaving or keeping her distance from the winner. Similarly, much negotiation ends with one side deciding to lump it instead of pursuing the claim. Or, rather than take a dispute to court or engage in coercive actions, one party (or both) may decide to break off the relationship altogether. This is common in social contexts where the disputant perceives satisfactory alternatives to the relationship.

Lumping it and avoidance may also occur before a claim has been made, thus forestalling a dispute. Faced with the problem of stolen boots, the miner might have decided to lump it and not make a claim for the boots. More drastically, in a fit of exasperation, he might have walked off the job and never returned.

Which Approach Is "Best"?

When the mine superintendent described the boots dispute to us, he expressed a preference for how to resolve disputes. In our language, he was saying that on the whole it was better to try to reconcile interests than to focus on who was right or who was more powerful. But what does "better" mean? And in what sense, if any, was he correct in believing that focusing attention on interests is better?

What "Better" Means: Four Possible Criteria

The different approaches to the resolution of disputes—interests, rights, and power—generate different costs and benefits. We focus on four criteria in comparing them: transaction costs, satisfaction with outcomes, effect on the relationship, and recurrence of disputes.[11]

Transaction Costs. For the mine superintendent, "better" meant resolving disputes without strikes. More generally, he wanted to minimize the costs of disputing—what may be called the transaction costs. The most obvious costs of striking were economic. The management payroll and the overhead costs had to be met while the mine stood idle. Sometimes strikes led to violence and the destruction of company property. The miners, too, incurred costs—lost wages. Then there were the lost opportunities for the company: a series of strikes could lead to the loss of a valuable sales contract. In a family argument, the costs would include the frustrating hours spent disputing, the frayed nerves and tension headaches, and the missed opportunities to do more enjoyable or useful tasks. All dispute resolution procedures carry transaction costs: the time, money, and emotional energy expended in disputing; the resources consumed and destroyed; and the opportunities lost.[12]

Satisfaction with Outcomes. Another way to evaluate different approaches to dispute resolution is by the parties' mutual satisfaction with the result. The outcome of the strike could not have been wholly satisfactory to the miner—he did not receive new boots—but he did succeed in venting his frustration and taking his revenge. A disputant's satisfaction depends largely on how much the resolution fulfills the interests that led her to make or reject the claim in the first place.

Satisfaction may also depend on whether the disputant believes that the resolution is fair. Even if an agreement does not wholly fulfill her interests, a disputant may draw some satisfaction from the resolution's fairness.

Satisfaction depends not only on the perceived fairness of the resolution, but also on the perceived fairness of the dispute resolution procedure. Judgments about fairness turn on several factors: how much opportunity a disputant had to express himself; whether he had control over accepting or rejecting the settlement; how much he was able to participate in shaping the settlement; and whether he believes that the third party, if there was one, acted fairly.[13]

Effect on the Relationship. A third criterion is the long-term effect on the parties' relationship. The approach taken to resolve a dispute may affect the parties' ability to work together on a day-to-day basis. Constant quarrels with threats of divorce may seriously weaken a marriage. In contrast, marital counseling in which the disputing partners learn to focus on interests in order to resolve disputes may strengthen a marriage.

Recurrence. The final criterion is whether a particular approach produces durable resolutions. The simplest form of recurrence is when a resolution fails to stick. For example, a dispute between father and teenage son over curfew appears resolved but breaks out again and again. A subtler form of recurrence takes place when a resolution is reached in a particular dispute, but the resolution fails to prevent the same dispute from arising between one of the disputants and someone else, or conceivably between two different parties in the same community. For instance, a man guilty of sexually harassing an employee reaches an agreement with his victim that is satisfactory to her, but he continues to harass other women employees. Or he stops, but other men continue to harass women employees in the same organization.

The Relationship Among the Four Criteria. These four different criteria are interrelated. Dissatisfaction with outcomes may produce strain on the relationship, which contributes to the recurrence of disputes, which in turn increases transaction costs. Because the different costs typically increase and decrease together, it is convenient to refer to all four together as the costs of disputing. When we refer to a particular approach as "high-cost" or "low-cost," we mean not just transaction costs but also dissatisfaction with outcomes, strain on the relationship, and recurrence of disputes.

Sometimes one cost can be reduced only by increasing another, particularly in the short term. If father and son sit down to discuss their conflicting interests concerning curfew, the short-term transaction costs in terms of time and energy may be high. Still, these costs may be more than offset by the benefits of a successful negotiation—an improved relationship and the cessation of curfew violations.

Which Approach Is Least Costly?

Now that we have defined "better" in terms of the four types of costs, the question remains whether the mine superintendent was right in supposing that focusing on interests is better. A second question is also important: when an interests-based approach fails, is it less costly to focus on rights or on power?

Interests Versus Rights or Power. A focus on interests can resolve the problem underlying the dispute more effectively than can a focus on rights or power. An example is a grievance filed against a mine foreman for doing work that contractually only a miner is authorized to do. Often the real problem is something else—a miner who feels unfairly assigned to an unpleasant task may file a grievance only to strike back at his foreman. Clearly, focusing on what the contract says about foremen working will not deal with this underlying problem. Nor will striking to protest foremen working. But if the foreman and miner can negotiate about the miner's future work tasks, the dispute may be resolved to the satisfaction of both.

Just as an interests-based approach can help uncover hidden problems, it can help the parties identify which issues are of greater concern to one than to the other. By trading off issues of lesser concern for those of greater concern, both parties can gain from the resolution of the dispute.[14] Consider, for example, a union and employer negotiating over two issues: additional vacation time and flexibility of work assignments. Although the union does not like the idea of assignment flexibility, its clear priority is additional vacation. Although the employer does not like the idea of additional vacation, he cares more about gaining flexibility in assigning work. An agreement that gives the union the vacation days it seeks and the employer flexibility in making work assignments would likely be satisfactory to both. Such joint gain is more likely to be realized if the parties focus on each side's interests. Focusing on who is right, as in litigation, or on who is more powerful, as in a strike, usually leaves at least one party perceiving itself as the loser.

Reconciling interests thus tends to generate a higher level of mutual satisfaction with outcomes than determining rights or power.[15] If the parties are more satisfied, their relationship benefits, and the dispute is less likely to recur. Determining who is right or who is more powerful, with the emphasis on winning and losing, typically makes the relationship more adversarial and strained. Moreover, the loser frequently does not give up, but appeals to a higher court or plots revenge. To be sure, reconciling interests can sometimes take a long time, especially when there are many parties to the dispute. Generally, however, these costs pale in comparison with the transaction costs of rights and power contests such as trials, hostile corporate takeovers, or wars.

In sum, focusing on interests, compared to focusing on rights or power, tends to produce higher satisfaction with outcomes, better working relationships and less recurrence, and may also incur lower transaction costs. As a rough generalization, then, an interests approach is less costly than a rights or power approach.

Rights Versus Power. Although determining who is right or who is more powerful can strain the relationship, deferring to a fair standard usually takes less of a toll than giving in to a threat. In a dispute between a father and teenager over curfew, a discussion of independent standards such as the curfews of other teenagers is likely to strain the relationship less than an exchange of threats.

Determining rights or power frequently becomes a contest—a competition among the parties to determine who will prevail. They may compete with words to persuade a third-party decision maker of the merits of their case, as in adjudication; or they may compete with actions intended to show the other who is more powerful, as in a proxy fight. Rights contests differ from power contests chiefly in their transaction costs. A power contest typically costs more in resources consumed and opportunities lost. Strikes cost more than arbitration. Violence costs more than litigation. The high transaction costs stem not only from the efforts invested in the fight but also from the destruction of each side's resources. Destroying the opposition may be the very object of a power contest. Moreover, power contests often create new injuries and new disputes along with anger, distrust, and a desire for revenge. Power contests, then, typically damage the relationship more and lead to greater recurrence of disputes than do rights contests. In general, a rights approach is less costly than a power approach.

Proposition

To sum up, we argue that, in general, reconciling interests is less costly than determining who is right, which in turn is less costly than determining who is more powerful. This proposition does not mean that focusing on interests is invariably better than focusing on rights and power, but simply means that it tends to result in lower transaction costs, greater satisfaction with outcomes, less strain on the relationship, and less recurrence of disputes.

Focusing on Interests Is Not Enough

Despite these general advantages, resolving *all* disputes by reconciling interests alone is neither possible nor desirable. It is useful to consider why.

When Determining Rights or Power Is Necessary

In some instances, interests-based negotiation cannot occur unless rights or power procedures are first employed to bring a recalcitrant party to the negotiating table. An environmental group, for example, may file a lawsuit against a developer to bring about a negotiation. A community group may organize a demonstration on the steps of the town hall to get the mayor to discuss its interests in improving garbage collection service.

In other disputes, the parties cannot reach agreement on the basis of interests because their perceptions of who is right or who is more powerful are so different that they cannot establish a range in which to negotiate. A rights procedure may be needed to clarify the rights boundary within which a negotiated resolution can be sought. If a discharged employee and her employer (as well as their lawyers) have very different estimations about whether a court would award damages to the employee, it will be difficult for them to negotiate a settlement. Nonbinding arbitration may clarify the parties' rights and allow them to negotiate a resolution.

Just as uncertainty about the rights of the parties will sometimes make negotiation difficult, so too will uncertainty about their relative power. When one party in an ongoing relationship wants to demonstrate that the balance of power has shifted in its favor, it may find that only a power contest will adequately make the point. It is a truism among labor relations practitioners that a conflict-ridden union-management relationship often settles down after a lengthy strike. The strike reduces uncertainty about the relative power of the parties that had made each party unwilling to concede. Such long-term benefits sometimes justify the high transaction costs of a power contest.

In some disputes, the interests are so opposed that agreement is not possible. Focusing on interests cannot resolve a dispute between a right-to-life group and an abortion clinic over whether the clinic will continue to exist. Resolution will likely be possible only through a rights contest, such as a trial, or a power contest, such as a demonstration or a legislative battle.

When Are Rights or Power Procedures Desirable?

Although reconciling interests is generally less costly than determining rights, only adjudication can authoritatively resolve questions of public importance. If the 1954 Supreme Court case, *Brown* v. *Board of Education* (347 U.S. 483), outlawing racial segregation in public schools, had been resolved by negotiation rather than by adjudication, the immediate result might have been the same—the black plaintiff would have attended an all-white Topeka, Kansas public school. The societal impact, however, would have been far less significant. As it was, *Brown* laid the groundwork for the elimination of racial segregation in all of American public life. In at least some cases, then, rights-based court procedures are preferable, from a societal perspective, to resolution through interests-based negotiation.[16]

Some people assert that a powerful party is ill-advised to focus on interests when dealing regularly with a weaker party. But even if one party is more powerful, the costs of imposing one's will can be high. Threats must be backed up with actions from time to time. The weaker party may fail to fully comply with a resolution based on power, thus requiring the more powerful party to engage in expensive policing. The weaker party may also take revenge—in small ways, perhaps, but nonetheless a nuisance. And revenge may be quite costly to the more powerful if the power balance ever shifts, as it can quite unexpectedly, or if the weaker party's cooperation is ever needed in another domain. Thus, for a more powerful party, a focus on interests, within the bounds set by power, may be more desirable than would appear at first glance.

Low-Cost Ways to Determine Rights and Power

Because focusing on rights and power plays an important role in effective dispute resolution, differentiating rights and power procedures on the basis of costs is useful. We distinguish three types of rights and power procedures: negotiation, low-cost contests, and high-cost contests. Rights-based negotiation is typically less costly than a rights contest such as court or arbitration. Similarly, power-based negotiation, marked by threats, typically costs less than a power contest in which those threats are carried out.

Different kinds of contests incur different costs. If arbitration dispenses with procedures typical of a court trial (extensive discovery, procedural motions, and lengthy briefs), it can be much cheaper than going to court. In a fight, shouting is less costly than physical assault. A strike in which workers refuse only overtime work is less costly than a full strike.

The Goal:
An Interests-Oriented Dispute Resolution System

Not all disputes can be—or should be—resolved by reconciling interests. Rights and power procedures can sometimes accomplish what interests-based procedures cannot. The problem is that rights and power procedures are often used where they are not necessary. A procedure that should be the last resort too often becomes the first resort. The goal, then, is a dispute resolution system that looks like the pyramid on the right in Figure 2: most disputes are resolved through reconciling interests, some through determining who is right, and the fewest through determining who is more powerful. By contrast, a distressed dispute resolution system would look like the inverted pyramid on the left in Figure 2. Comparatively few disputes are resolved through reconciling interests, while many are resolved through determining rights and power. The challenge for the systems designer is to turn the pyramid right side up. It is to design a system that promotes the reconciling of interests but that also provides low-cost ways to determine rights or power for those disputes that cannot or should not be resolved by focusing on interests alone. The chapters that follow discuss how a designer might go about creating such a system.

**Figure 2. Moving from a Distressed to an Effective
Dispute Resolution System.**

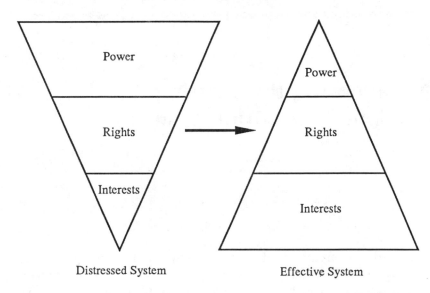

Distressed System   Effective System

Chapter 2

❖❖

Diagnosing the Existing
Dispute Resolution System

In order to create an effective dispute resolution system, the designer should first carefully diagnose the existing system. The designer needs to know what kinds of disputes occur, what procedures are being used, and why the parties are using one procedure rather than another. Diagnosis is essential, since changes are unlikely to work unless they satisfy the needs that lead the parties to use existing procedures.

At one large American corporation, lawyers and managers periodically review recent legal disputes in order to predict what type of disputes are likely to arise in the future, and to determine whether less costly and more satisfactory procedures might be used.[1] In a limited fashion, they are doing what we call a "dispute resolution diagnosis." This sensible practice can usefully be expanded and extended to all kinds of organizations and relationships. Lawyers could sit down with their clients, unions with management, partners in a joint venture with each other, American arms control negotiators with Soviet negotiators—all could review their disputes and grievances, past and ongoing, in order to assess how they are being handled and at what cost.

A dispute resolution diagnosis seeks the answers to three questions:

1. *What* are the current and recent issues in dispute? Who are the parties? How many disputes occur? The answers to these questions suggest the kind and number of disputes that the dispute resolution system will have to handle in the future.
2. *How* are disputes being handled? What types of dispute resolution procedures are being used and with what frequency? What are the overall costs and benefits of these procedures? The answers provide a map of the existing procedures from which the designer can work.
3. *Why* are particular procedures being used and not others? What functions are served by court, power contests, and other high-cost procedures? What obstacles hinder the use of interests-based negotiation? If interests-based negotiation is to become the norm, it must serve those functions and overcome those obstacles.

This chapter is structured around these three questions—what, how, and why, using as the primary illustration our 1980 intervention at the strike-torn Caney Creek mine (described in detail in Chapter Six). We focus first on diagnosing the dispute resolution system in an existing organization or relationship; at the end of the chapter, we discuss doing a diagnosis in a new organization or relationship. We begin by offering a model of a dispute resolution system.

An Overview of the Model

As depicted in Figure 3, the central feature of a dispute resolution system is the procedures used for resolving disputes. The input is disputes. The output is costs and benefits: transaction costs, level of satisfaction with the outcomes, impact on the relationship, and the frequency with which disputes recur. Four main factors directly affect the procedures in use: the procedures available, the parties' motivations, the parties' skills, and the resources available. The dispute resolution system serves an organization or relationship, which in turn exists in a larger social, economic, and cultural environment, all of which indirectly affect the procedures used.

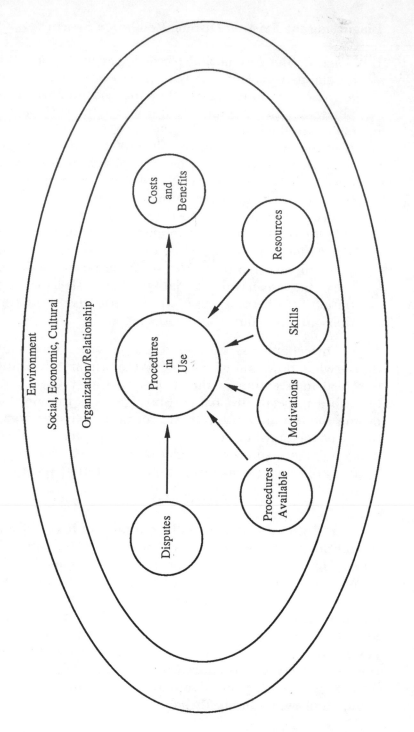

Figure 3. Model of a Dispute Resolution System.

Let us take Caney Creek as an illustration. The issue most commonly producing disputes at Caney Creek was the allocation of jobs; the principal parties were miners and management. The *procedures in use* focused mostly on rights and power. Interests-based negotiation took place rarely, if at all. Miners frequently lumped it. There was a good deal of rights-based negotiation and frequent arbitration. Wildcat strikes were common, averaging more than one a month. The resulting costs, not surprisingly, were high—hundreds of thousands of dollars in lost wages and production, a high degree of dissatisfaction with the outcomes of disputes, a strained relationship on the verge of total breakdown, and frequently recurring disputes.

At Caney Creek, the *procedures available* for dealing with disputes included the four-step grievance procedure prescribed by the national collective bargaining contract as well as the wildcat strike—the power procedure traditionally used by coal miners. The miners' *motivation* to strike frequently outweighed their motivation to use the contractual grievance procedure. While strikes rarely produced a satisfactory outcome, at least they provided an opportunity to vent emotions and take revenge. Moreover, the parties lacked problem-solving and listening *skills*, making it almost impossible to negotiate difficult, emotionally laden disputes. Few *resources* were available for interests-based dispute resolution. There were no natural third parties who could mediate between union and management, nor was there a manager whose primary responsibility was labor relations.

This distressed dispute resolution system served a *relationship* between two organizations, union and management. The characteristics of these organizations affected the procedures used; for example, neither union leaders nor managers were selected for or trained in problem-solving skills. The relationship in turn was embedded in a larger economic, social, cultural, and political *environment*. The surrounding Appalachian culture, with its emphasis on fighting for one's rights, reinforced the tendencies to engage in rights and power procedures. Given these procedures, skills, motivations,

and resources—as well as the organization and environment—
it is little wonder that interests-based negotiation was less
used at Caney Creek than arbitration and wildcat strikes.

The three diagnostic questions—what, how, and why—
relate to the model depicted in Figure 3 as follows: the *what*
question focuses on the disputes. The *how* question identifies
the procedures in use and their costs and benefits. The *why*
question focuses primarily on the four factors that directly
affect the procedures in use, but also includes the impact of
the organization (or relationship) and the environment.

What Are the Disputes About?

A designer asks such questions as:

- Who are the disputants? Who are other important players
  in the disputes? At Bryant High School in New York,
  troubled by tensions and violence, some disputes involved
  only students, others involved both students and teachers,
  and still others were between students and their parents.[2]
  The dispute resolution system designed for this high
  school was capable of involving all these actors. In other
  organizations, there may be different systems for disputes
  among different actors. For example, a corporation may
  have different systems for dealing with customer complaints, disputes with suppliers, employee grievances, disputes between departments, or problems that arise in joint
  ventures.
- What are the types of disputes? If disputes tend to have a
  strong emotional element, the designer should consider
  methods to vent emotions. If the disputes involve purely
  legal or technical issues, such as the price that Fujitsu
  must pay for the use of IBM software, a low-cost rights
  procedure might be most appropriate.
- How frequently do disputes occur? What does this suggest
  about the frequency of disputes in the future? In the IBM-
  Fujitsu controversy, hundreds of disputes over intellectual
  property rights had arisen, and there was every reason to
  think that hundreds more would arise in the future. The

transaction costs of resolving this volume of disputes through conventional rights procedures such as court or arbitration would have been enormous. This underscored the need for designing procedures that would both reduce the number of such disputes and resolve at low cost those that did arise.

- Are any changes expected in the organization or relationship or in the wider environment that would affect the number and nature of disputes? Increasing computerization of the workplace may stimulate new disputes over working conditions and over discharges of workers whose services are no longer needed. An economic recession may reduce profits, sharpening the clash of interests in disputes over wages and job security. New government regulations, such as a law prohibiting discrimination against AIDS victims, may create a new category of disputes. Such changes will affect people's interests, rights, or power. They may intensify opposed interests or create new interests altogether. By affecting people's perceptions of their rights or their relative power, they may give rise to new rights and power contests.

- What is causing the disputes? Sometimes identifying causes can suggest ways to prevent similar disputes in the future. If one cause of an overloaded employee grievance system is an overtime work policy, perceived as unjust, changing the policy could reduce the number of grievances. Often the causes of disputes are inherent conflicts of interest: the union wants more money for less work, management wants more work for less money; the sales division wants to offer more television models for sale, the manufacturing division wants to offer fewer. It is easy to mistake such disputes simply as personality clashes between key people. One designer described the frequent disputes that arose between the state level organization of a union and the largest local organization of that union:

A lot of it is blamed on personality. I think personalities play a role, but I also think the conflict is structural, because I've seen it in several states. The large local has got all kinds of benefits and so when the state organization wants to lobby the legislature for benefits, the large local doesn't want to participate. It's a tremendous conflict, but it often is framed in terms of personalities.[3]

How Are Disputes Handled?

In any organization or relationship, a variety of dispute resolution procedures are available. Disputes between husband and wife may be resolved through interests-based negotiation, threats and sulking, or the informal mediation of a friend. At the extreme is physical violence or divorce. Disputes between department heads in a corporation may be resolved through negotiation or may be turned over to a superior for decision. Disputes between towns and developers about the location of a hazardous waste site may be negotiated, adjudicated, or decided by vote in the legislature.

Often these different procedures are used simultaneously or in sequence. If the partners in a joint venture fail to settle a dispute through negotiation, they may go to court; while the lawsuit is pending, they may continue negotiations through their lawyers. Disputes between a husband and wife may routinely start with an argument about who is right, proceed to tense avoidance of the issue, then get reopened, and eventually be resolved by one side giving in. The next time a dispute arises between them, they follow the same pattern of behavior.

Sometimes procedural sequences are formally prescribed by law, contract, or organizational rules. For instance, if a threatened strike imperils the national health or safety, the Taft-Hartley Act provides that the President may appoint a board of inquiry, whose report is followed by an eighty-day court injunction against striking. During this time, the board of inquiry makes a second report, which is followed by a vote on whether to strike. Only then is a strike legal.[4] Many contracts mandate arbitration should negotiation fail to resolve a dispute about the meaning of the contract. Many companies have complaint procedures for their customers. Just because a procedure is formally prescribed, however, does not mean that it is used as intended—or even used at all.

Mapping Out the Procedures in Use

In order to get a full picture of how disputes are handled in a particular system, the designer maps out the procedures in use, those that are prescribed as well as those that are not. Failing to do so creates the risk that new procedures will be designed that function at cross-purposes with existing procedures. In mapping out the procedures in use, the designer seeks to identify the types of procedures used, their relative frequency, their regular sequence, if any, and the time taken for resolution. She asks questions such as:

- What do people do if they have a complaint? With whom, if anyone, do they bring it up? How frequently do they just lump it? In many marriages, for example, it is common for one or both partners to stifle minor complaints about the other's habits, thinking that no change will be forthcoming if they complain or fearing that a complaint will provoke an argument that will be destructive to their relationship.
- What happens when disputes are negotiated? What proportion are resolved this way? Do the parties search for settlements that will satisfy the interests of each? Or do they focus chiefly on their respective rights? Or are their negotiations dominated by threats, intimidation attempts, and other power tactics?
- How frequently do negotiations break down, and what happens when they do? Do the parties turn to others— lawyers, union officials, friends—for help in negotiating? Are disputes turned over to superiors for resolution? Do parties turn to a neutral person for mediation? Or are disputes dropped as one party (or both) lumps it?

- Are adjudicatory procedures available? What kinds? How often are they used, and how long does it take before a decision is reached? Does one party prevail most of the time?
- How often do power contests erupt? What types of power behavior are used? What outcomes result? Is there typically a winner, or does the power contest appear to serve no purpose beyond the release of pent-up anger and frustration?

Charting Common Sequences

From the information collected about procedures in use, the designer can begin to sort out common sequences and plot them on a type of flowchart. Let us take a hypothetical coal mine as an example. The mine has the four-step grievance procedure prescribed by the national collective bargaining contract. In step 1, a miner with a complaint brings it up with his immediate foreman. If not satisfied, in step 2 he asks the mine committee to discuss the grievance with mine management. In the absence of agreement at that level, a third meeting—step 3—is held with higher-level representatives of the union and management. If this too fails to resolve the dispute, it is submitted in step 4 to an arbitrator for decision.

Figure 4 illustrates our hypothetical map. The actual pattern of dispute resolution at the mine, as we discover through questions and observations, differs markedly from the prescribed procedures. In addition to the four-step grievance procedure, a miner perceives two alternatives: to lump it and to provoke a wildcat strike. From interviews with miners and management, we estimate that there have been approximately two hundred instances in the previous year in which a miner had a complaint. In half of these cases, the miner brought his complaint to his foreman; in nearly half, the miner lumped it; and in ten cases, the miner instigated a strike. Thus, half the time, the miners chose not to use the prescribed procedures.

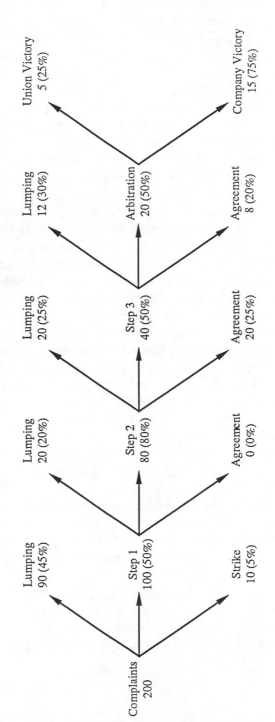

Figure 4. Flow Chart of Dispute Resolution at a Hypothetical Coal Mine.

Of the claims made to the foreman, none was settled at that level. Twenty percent were lumped; the remainder went on to step 2. One quarter of the step 2 negotiations resulted in agreement, another quarter ended in the miner lumping it, and half were referred to step 3. At step 3, agreements were reached only in a fifth of the disputes, half went on to arbitration; and the remainder were lumped. The miners won 25 percent of the cases that went to arbitration; the company won 75 percent. Further questioning reveals that although some step 2 negotiations were interests-based, most were rights-based, and that step 3 negotiations were almost entirely rights-based.

This map reveals a good deal about dispute resolution at this mine. There appears to be a low level of confidence in the prescribed procedures, with 50 percent of all complaints being lumped or leading to a strike even before the procedures are tried. While some lumping is normal, the frequency here suggests considerable dissatisfaction with the prescribed procedures. Step 1 appears to be a means of presenting claims and no more—no agreements were reached. Step 2 produced some agreements, mostly when an interests-based approach was used. Also noticeable is the substantial amount of lumping it after both steps 2 and 3. Many miners appear to believe that if agreement is not reached at step 2, there is little to be gained at step 3 or arbitration. Finally, arbitration decisions are one-sided. Whatever the reason—weak cases being taken to arbitration, unskilled advocates, or biased arbitrators—it is not surprising that the miners have little confidence in arbitration.

In sum, the map shows a system in distress: lots of lumping it and power contests instead of negotiation, no negotiated settlements early on at step 1, few at step 3, and an arbitration procedure where the results are one-sided. The only small measure of success is step 2; the occasional use of an interests-based approach there could provide an important starting point in the design of an improved system. Such an exercise shows the "gaps" in the system: in this case, the comparative absence of interests-based procedures and the gap between the prescribed procedures and the procedures in use.

Assessing the Costs

The information collected about the type, duration, and frequency of the procedures used should make it possible to estimate the costs of dispute resolution. Since the designer's goal is to reduce these costs, it is important to know what they are at the start. This will allow the designer to judge how well the design changes are working and make adjustments accordingly. The questions to determine cost are straightforward:

- How long do the various procedures take, and how much money is consumed by them?
- How satisfied are disputants with the outcomes of disputes?
- What effect do existing procedures have on personal or organizational relationships?
- How often do the same disputes recur because they were never actually resolved?

The designer may feel tempted to cut short the time spent documenting the costs of the existing procedures, especially when the relationship is obviously distressed and the parties are eager for a quick fix. It should be remembered, however, that systematic documentation of the results of the designer's work can be useful to persuade the parties to continue with changed procedures or to persuade other parties to try similar changes. This was the case with the grievance mediation program: careful evaluation helped spread grievance mediation to new mines and to other industries.

Why Are Disputes Handled This Way?

Why are people resorting to rights and power contests instead of negotiating more? Possible reasons include lack of interests-based negotiation procedures, lack of motivation to use them, lack of skills, lack of resources, and obstacles in the organization, relationship, or the larger environment.

Lack of Procedures

In any organization or relationship, certain dispute resolution procedures are available. They may be customary, as in the case of strikes, or they may be formally provided by the larger community, as in the case of courts. They may be procedures agreed upon by the parties or their representatives, as in the case of the contractual grievance procedure in the unionized coal industry; or they may be made available by one party, as in the case of a company's customer complaint procedure.

In some situations, procedures prescribed by law, contract, or organizational rules exist only for certain types of claims. Other claims are ignored, producing frustration that occasionally erupts in a costly power contest. At Caney Creek, for example, a negotiating procedure existed only for disputes about the interpretation of the contract. No established procedures existed for interpersonal disputes or for those that concerned noncontractual issues of fairness. In other situations, no interests-based procedures have been established. For Bryant High students involved in disputes with teachers, administrators, parents, or fellow students, there was no place to turn for problem-solving mediation. For environmental groups opposed to the plans of developers and highway builders, the most commonly used procedure until recent years was litigation; problem-solving negotiation was virtually unknown.

People and organizations involved in a dispute do not necessarily need a prescribed procedure to engage in interests-based negotiation, but such a procedure can help. It can make interests-based negotiation a prominent alternative, and keep disputes from escalating to rights and power contests. This suggests some questions for the designer to ask:

- Are interests-based procedures available to handle the full range of disputes that occur?
- Are some disputes being lumped simply because no established procedure exists to deal with them?
- Does a mediation procedure exist that focuses on interests?

Lack of Motivation

Even with a negotiation procedure in place, the parties may lack the motivation to negotiate. At Caney Creek, miners were reluctant to raise problems with their foremen for fear of retaliation. Moreover, the grievance procedure was regarded with skepticism. Outcomes were rarely if ever satisfactory to the miners, and many felt deprived of their "voice" in the dispute. At step 3 and arbitration the miner was a passive observer, while union and company representatives argued about contractual technicalities far removed from the actual problem as the miner perceived it. Arbitration decisions, often handed down many months after the grievance was first raised, would more often than not deny the grievance, sometimes in language incomprehensible to miners. Any miner, in contrast, could instigate a wildcat strike and receive immediate attention. Even if he did not win the grievance, his voice would be heard, and he would receive the emotional satisfaction of revenge. Thus, the motivation to strike outweighed the motivation to use the grievance procedure.

Exploring the motivations that lie behind the use of different procedures is a key task for the designer. It helps to identify obstacles to negotiation that should be removed, and it highlights the need for positive incentives. Just as important, it serves to identify the perceived benefits provided by rights and power contests. These same benefits may need to be matched if disputants are to use lower-cost procedures instead. Curtailing the strikes at Caney Creek, for instance, would require an alternative procedure that allowed the miner to vent his anger and to voice his grievance in his own terms. In exploring disputants' motivation to use a procedure, the designer might ask such questions as:

- How satisfied are disputants with the outcomes of the procedure?
- Does the procedure provide an opportunity for "voice"? Can disputants air their grievances fully in their own terms? Do disputants have control over the procedure—

are they in charge, or does someone take it out of their hands? Do disputants participate in shaping the outcome? Do they think the procedure is fair?

- Does the procedure allow for the venting of emotions such as anger and frustration? Is it a way of getting revenge? How much do people simply enjoy fighting for its own sake? As a schoolgirl at Bryant High put it, "All I ever wanted to do was fight. If someone said something to me I didn't like, I didn't think about talking, I just thought about fighting."[5]
- How costly do disputants perceive the procedure to be in terms of time and money?
- Does the procedure serve the interests of parties other than the disputants? A strike that is ostensibly called in support of a grievance may actually be intended to benefit the union leadership by focusing attention on the company as a common enemy, thus solidifying the union internally. Alternatively, strikes may be instigated by opponents of the union leadership to undermine the authority of leaders who have asked the members not to strike.
- Does the procedure serve purposes for the disputants other than resolving the particular dispute at hand? A company may file a series of lawsuits to impose costs on another company; a union may file a series of grievances to make a new personnel director look bad; one government may negotiate with another not to resolve a dispute but to impress the public.

Knowing what motivates the parties to use high-cost procedures is crucial for the designer who seeks a better system. This is not to suggest that the parties to a particular dispute always choose a procedure only after careful weighing of the possible costs and benefits. In many cases, the immediate motivation for using a particular procedure might be nothing more than sheer habit and custom: "That's the way it's done around here." In order to persuade the parties to break away from costly habits or customs, however, the designer must get them to focus on the costs and benefits of the procedures they are using to resolve disputes compared to those of alternative procedures.

Lack of Skill

At Bryant High School, one obstacle to the use of problem-solving negotiation was lack of skill among disputants. The same was true at Caney Creek, where we found that key managers and union officials had poor communication and negotiation skills.

Even where skills are adequate, the parties' belief to the contrary may deter them from using an interests-based procedure. One designer who works with a teachers' union and various school boards told us:

> I was surprised to find union and management representatives reluctant to use grievance mediation even though they had previously used mediation in contract negotiations. Informal discussions with them brought me to the realization that they feared their skills were inadequate. They viewed mediation of contract negotiations as being rather simple since they would typically have several issues to discuss, some of which they could trade off and others they could discard. They were uncertain what would happen in grievance mediation, particularly since they viewed a grievance as a single issue and they would have nothing to trade off or discard.[6]

The purpose of assessing dispute resolution skills and knowledge is to determine whether training or coaching would help. The kinds of questions the designer might ask are:

- Do people know what procedures are available and when? Do they know what they are expected to do in the procedures? Do they know how to use the procedures to generate a satisfactory resolution?

- How skilled are disputants and their representatives in problem-solving negotiation? How good are they at listening to each other, probing for interests, and exploring creative options?
- How skilled are disputants and their representatives in presenting their case in arbitration? Do they make the appropriate arguments? Are they presenting their evidence effectively?

Diagnosis of skills is particularly useful when the behavior of key individuals may be a primary reason for frequent disputes. One question that arises in such cases is whether to train or replace the individuals. This was the dilemma we faced at Caney Creek with the mine foreman and the local union president, the two people most directly responsible for the grievance procedure. Neither was particularly skilled at problem solving, and disputes tended to escalate rapidly into heated arguments. We knew that their antagonism derived in part from the roles they played. We also learned, however, that this level of conflict between mine and local union officials was unusual, that their interpersonal animosity extended back for years, and that it resulted from incidents that occurred outside the mine. We concluded that trying to enhance their skills would probably not succeed in increasing the use of problem-solving negotiations at the mine; one or both of them needed to be replaced.

Lack of Resources

Even if interests-based negotiation procedures are available, their use may be hampered by a lack of the people, information, or institutions that make them work effectively.

A frequently missing resource is people who are available to help disputants resolve their disputes. For example, at Caney Creek, there was no one in management whose primary job was labor relations. Grievances were handled by a mine foreman whose chief responsibility was operations and who had neither the time, the training, nor the inclination to

take a problem-solving approach. Other organizations or relationships lack neutrals, such as mediators and arbitrators, or
people to administer court resolution procedures.

A second important resource is information. For example, the provision of information concerning prior settlements
has greatly facilitated the settlement of claims by victims of
asbestosis.[7] Information may also include technical information about the problem. A third needed resource is an
institution to provide people and information. For example,
mediators of international disputes often have nowhere to
turn for advice, skills training, detailed knowledge about the
conflict, funds, and staff assistance. No international mediation service exists to assist them.[8]

The designer should ask these questions in diagnosing
resources:

- Are there people to whom disputants can turn for help—
  people to represent them, give them advice, or serve as
  mediators or arbitrators?
- How skilled are these representatives, mediators, or arbitrators? Are the neutrals perceived as fair and unbiased?
- Is negotiation hampered by a lack of norms, precedents,
  laws, and other standards that could be used to settle
  disputes or by a lack of technical information about the
  problem?
- Do the procedures need to be actively administered by
  a person or an institution? Is an institution needed to
  provide people and information on an ongoing basis?
- Is a lack of people, information, or institutions due to
  insufficient funding?

Obstacles in the Organization and Environment

In working on the dispute resolution system in a large
high-tech organization,[9] one designer discovered a persistent
pattern of avoiding disputes. Managers failed to confront differences over budget and project authority, putting off dealing
with problems until they became major crises; then the com-

pany president would decide the outcome. Frustrated managers were leaving the organization. The pattern of handling disputes was taking a high toll in performance and morale.

The designer discovered two major obstacles to effective dispute resolution. First was the organization's highly centralized decision-making structure. New managers rapidly discovered that the president reserved primary authority for all decisions and that they would be rewarded not for negotiating resolutions to their disputes but rather for deferring to the president's wishes. The second obstacle was the cultural background—the beliefs and practices—of the senior managers, including the president. Their culture stressed appearance of harmony, avoidance of confrontation, and deference to authority.

As the example illustrates, diagnosis seeks to uncover the ways that the organization and its environment produce and reinforce a particular pattern of dispute resolution. Occasionally the diagnosis can lead to practical suggestions for changing organizational policies or for circumventing environmental obstacles. Perhaps its most important purpose is to highlight obstacles that may make certain procedures impractical. The diagnosis above, for instance, led the designer to conclude that in order to make significant changes, she would have to involve the company president and confront the cultural barriers to dealing with conflict.

Questions for the designer to ask might include:

- In what ways are procedures in use affected by organizational decision-making procedures? How centralized are these procedures? In the example above, the company's highly centralized decision making inhibited negotiation at lower levels.
- How are procedures in use affected by the organization's formal and informal reward systems? What kind of dispute resolution behavior is rewarded by superiors? By peers? For example, in the company discussed above, superiors and peers rewarded managers who avoided open discussion of disputes and left their resolution to the president.

- What impact does the personnel selection and training system have on the dispute resolution system? At Caney Creek, for instance, managers were neither selected for nor trained in problem-solving skills.
- How does the surrounding culture affect the procedures used? For instance, in the subculture of coal mining, striking is an honored tradition and is supported by the custom of showing solidarity with fellow union members.

A Dispute Resolution Diagnosis for New Relationships

When designing a system for a new organization or relationship, such as when lawyers draft a contractual dispute resolution clause, it is useful to ask the same diagnostic questions: what, how, and why. The difference is that instead of diagnosing past and current attempts at dispute resolution, one tries to anticipate how future disputes will likely be handled in the absence of a design effort. Central to such diagnosis is understanding the experience of similar organizations or relationships.

Suppose, for example, that a new health maintenance organization (HMO) is being established. The director of client relations must design a system for resolving potential disputes between subscribers and the HMO. She should start by asking *what* types of disputes might be anticipated and in what numbers. What has been the experience of existing HMOs? Is there legislation on the horizon that might affect the number or type of disputes? She should then consider *how* such disputes have been handled: what procedures have existing HMOs established, and what have been their costs and benefits? She would want to know to what extent subscribers to other HMOs use other options, such as lumping it, going to court, or taking their business elsewhere. Finally, she should investigate *why:* what motivations, skills, and resources are likely to influence the parties' choice of procedures to resolve disputes? What is likely to be the impact of the organization or relationship or the environment in which it is embedded? For example, if HMO administrators are rewarded for following rules strictly, that may be a potential obstacle to creative interests-based negotiation.[10] Thorough diagnosis, then, can be just as useful when designing a system for a new relationship or organization as when improving an existing system.

What Diagnosis Offers

Diagnosis first establishes *what* kinds of disputes are likely to arise, how often, and between whom. Second, it identifies *how* disputes are being handled and where lower-cost procedures might be used. A diagnosis also gives the designer a base line of current disputing costs against which to judge the effect of the design changes. Perhaps most important, diagnosis reveals *why* particular procedures are being used. It explores the motivations that lie behind the use of procedures and the benefits that interests-based procedures must match if they are to take hold. It determines whether people need to be trained, coached, or in some instances, replaced. Finally, it examines the resources—people, information, and institutions—available to assist the disputants and determines whether they need to be supplemented. Armed with this information, the designer is ready to embark on designing a new or improved system. That is the subject of the next chapter.

❖❖

Chapter 3

Designing an Effective
Dispute Resolution System

Two oil companies, about to engage in a joint venture, agree in advance on a dispute resolution system. They will try to resolve all disputes in a partnership committee. Failing that, they will refer disputes to two senior executives, one from each company, both uninvolved in the joint venture. The executives' task is to study the problem and, in consultation with their respective companies, to negotiate a settlement. They thus act as mediators as well as negotiators. If the "wise counselors" cannot reach an agreement, the dispute will be sent to arbitration. Litigation will be avoided.[1]

A statewide fire fighters union and an organization of cities and towns in the state are unhappy with the delay, unsatisfactory outcomes, and damaged relationships resulting from state-mandated arbitration to resolve disputes about the terms of fire fighters' collective bargaining contracts. They consult a dispute systems designer, who proposes that a joint committee of labor and management officials use mediation to break impasses. Both groups accept his proposal and successfully lobby the state legislature to add mediation to the statute. Arbitration remains available for disputes that cannot otherwise be resolved, but the favored procedure is to be mediation.[2]

41

At the Catholic Archdiocese of Chicago, school administrators, looking for better ways to resolve disputes about
teacher dismissals and student suspensions, designed a multistep dispute resolution procedure that requires negotiation
between disputing parties; provides advice from a school conflict management board composed of teachers, parents, and
principals from other schools; and offers the services of a
trained mediator.[3]

In each of these situations, a dispute resolution system
is designed to reduce the costs of handling disputes and to
produce more satisfying and durable resolutions. This chapter discusses how to design such a system—how to create an
interests-oriented system, starting from a diagnosis of the existing system as outlined in Chapter Two. This chapter presents
six basic principles of dispute systems design:

1. Put the focus on interests.
2. Build in "loop-backs" to negotiation.
3. Provide low-cost rights and power backups.
4. Build in consultation before, feedback after.
5. Arrange procedures in a low-to-high-cost sequence.
6. Provide the necessary motivation, skills, and resources.

Principle 1: Put the Focus on Interests

The first principle, the subject of Chapter One, is the
most fundamental: Create (or strengthen) ways of reconciling
the interests of the disputants. The model of a dispute resolution system presented in Chapter Two suggests four com-
plementary ways to do this: design procedures, strengthen
motivation, enhance skills, and provide resources.

Designing Procedures

Various procedures can put the focus on interests.
Bringing About Negotiation as Early as Possible. At
International Harvester during the 1950s and early 1960s,
the number of grievances and arbitrations skyrocketed. In

response, management and union introduced a new procedure: the oral handling of grievances at the lowest possible level. When an employee raised a complaint, every effort was made to resolve it on the spot that very day—even if it meant senior management and union officials coming down to the shop floor. As the manager of labor relations put it, "We don't want paper [written grievances] coming up in the organization, we want people going down; we want to avoid the litigation approach of the past and adopt a problem-solving attitude."[4] The results were impressive: the number of written grievances plummeted to almost zero. Union and management officials did not spend more time handling disputes; if anything, they spent slightly less time.[5] The International Harvester example shows the value of applying problem-solving negotiation to disputes as early as possible.

In the wildcat strike study described in Chapter Five, Brett and Goldberg found that superintendents at mines with few strikes spent far more time underground listening to miners' complaints and suggestions than did their counterparts at mines with many strikes. The lesson is clear: a manager who is accessible may be able to resolve a situation in interests terms before it escalates into a rights dispute or a strike. Simply hearing someone out and acknowledging the validity of the complaint can help defuse a grievance even if little can be done to redress it.

Establishing a Negotiation Procedure. An established negotiation procedure becomes increasingly useful as the number of parties to the dispute grows, the complexity of the issues increases, and the parties grow larger and more bureaucratic. Such a procedure will designate, for example, who will participate in the negotiation, when it must begin and end, and what happens if it is unsuccessful. Such negotiation procedures exist in a variety of realms, from collective bargaining between labor and management to negotiation of federal environmental and safety regulations.

One example is mandatory negotiation about the location of hazardous waste treatment facilities. The siting of such facilities is a recurring problem in many states, often resulting in extensive litigation, legislative battles, and even power contests. When faced with the decision of a state agency to place unwanted waste facilities in their community, some local residents have obstructed highways, threatened to dynamite existing facilities, and taken public officials hostage— all to vent their anger about policy-making processes that failed to adequately address their concerns. Faced with this recurrent problem, one state has provided for compulsory negotiation between a prospective developer and representatives of the community. The goal of the negotiation is to minimize the detrimental effects of the facility and to compensate the community for whatever damage or risk remains. In the event that interests-based negotiations fail to result in agreement, the state may compel arbitration.[6] The goal of the legislation, however, is to create a negotiation procedure focused on interests and thus to avoid not only arbitration but also costly litigation and power contests.

Federal agencies looking for better ways to deal with conflict over proposed federal regulations have come up with another creative way to substitute interests-based negotiation for litigation. Typically, an agency publishes a proposed rule, interested parties comment on it, and the agency then issues a final rule. All too often, parties dissatisfied with the rule challenge it in the courts. In an effort to reduce such litigation, some federal agencies have developed a new negotiated approach to making regulations (often referred to as "neg-reg") in which the agency and the affected parties participate in mediated negotiations designed to produce a consensus:[7]

> Together the parties explore their shared interests as well as differences of opinion, collaborate in gathering and analyzing technical information, generate options, and bargain and trade across these options according to their differing priorities. If a consensus is reached, it is published in the *Federal Register* as the agency's notice of proposed rulemaking, and then the conventional review and comment process takes

over. Because most of the parties likely to comment have already agreed on the notice of proposed rulemaking, the review period should be
uneventful. The prospects of subsequent litigation should be all but eliminated.[8]

Agencies using this procedure typically provide resources to support it, primarily third parties who coordinate
the negotiations and provide mediation services.[9]

Designing Multiple-Step Negotiation. In multistep procedures, a dispute that is not resolved at one level of the organizational hierarchy moves to progressively higher levels, with
different negotiators involved at each step. One example is the
contractual grievance procedure in the coal industry: step 1 is
negotiation between the miner and his foreman, step 2 is negotiation between the mine committee and mine management,
and step 3 is negotiation between the district union representative and senior management.

Multistep negotiation procedures, common in the
labor-management context, are increasingly being used by
parties to long-term business contracts. One such procedure
was described by an attorney who frequently uses it:

> Lower-level business people—such as proj-
> ect managers from each organization who relate
> to each other on a day-to-day basis—try to resolve
> [the dispute]. If they can't, the dispute is passed
> up to their superiors. If the superiors can't resolve
> it, the dispute goes up to a vice-president, a senior
> vice-president, or the CEO, depending on the size
> of the company. The forces at work here are
> (1) You don't want your boss to know you failed
> to solve a problem, and (2) the people at the
> higher levels tend to have a broader perspective
> than the day-to-day operating people do.[10]

Another example of multistep negotiation is the "wise
counselor" procedure used in the oil industry and described

at the beginning of the chapter. An even broader perspective is achieved because the two "wise counselors," senior executives from each company, are deliberately selected for their detachment from the particular dispute. Using "wise counselors" is the closest one can come to involving a mediator without actually doing so.

In adding more negotiation steps, however, the designer needs to be careful. In some cases, the easy availability of a higher-level person will simply discourage people from reaching agreement at a lower level and will thus make lower-level negotiation a pro forma step.

Strengthening Motivation

Interests-based negotiation is inherently motivating. It tends to provide more satisfying outcomes, more voice, and more sense of control and does so at lower transaction costs than procedures such as litigation or power contests. However, there are frequently obstacles, specific to the situation, that discourage parties from using interests-based negotiation. These obstacles can often be surmounted with the appropriate design.

Creating Multiple Points of Entry. A person with a claim to make may not trust or feel a rapport with the person with whom she should raise the claim. This problem can be alleviated by providing multiple points of entry into the dispute resolution system. At the Massachusetts Institute of Technology, for instance, a student with a grievance can bring it up with the dean of students, the head of the academic department, a university administrator, or an ombudsman.[11] At IBM, an employee can raise a problem with his manager, his manager's superior, or, for personnel decisions, even the president of the company.[12]

Providing a Negotiator with Authority. At Caney Creek, miners were lumping many of their complaints, storing them up until they would erupt in a strike. Miners told us that it was not worth raising a grievance with their foreman since he had no authority to resolve it. Two approaches to this problem are possible: provide the foreman with the necessary authority, or offer the employee the opportunity to take his complaint to someone with authority. The first approach, decentralizing authority, is no small task; it may require significant organizational change. We suggested this approach at Caney Creek, but it was not carried out. At International Harvester, the second approach was taken: those with authority to settle the grievance came to the shop floor.

Stopping Retaliation. At Caney Creek, miners were reluctant to use the established negotiation procedure because it was generally perceived as an adversarial act, and many miners feared retaliation from their foremen. To allay this fear, management issued a call for miners to bring up their grievances and a public warning that any foreman found retaliating against an employee for filing a grievance would be discharged.

Providing Opportunities to Meet. Sometimes disputants fear suggesting negotiations will convey an impression of weakness. One way to deal with this problem is to provide for mandatory negotiations. Judges do this when they schedule pretrial settlement conferences. Another way is to provide occasions to meet, not explicitly for negotiation but at which negotiations can easily take place. The United Nations serves this purpose for dozens of disputing nations and groups for whom the risks of a formal meeting are too high. The cloakroom in the United States Senate serves a similar purpose, providing informal and private opportunities for senators to resolve their legislative disagreements. The systems designer can provide such occasions for informal interaction by, for example, encouraging managers to wander around the plant, organizing meetings on a topic of mutual interest, or even arranging a regular social gathering.

Providing Skills and Resources

In addition to strengthening the motivation to negotiate, a designer can encourage interests-based negotiation by providing for ongoing training and coaching in negotiation skills. Initial coaching can be provided by the designer and subsequent coaching by people such as a personnel director or union steward. These topics are dealt with in more detail in Chapter Four.

Providing a Person to Turn to for Help. The designer can also ensure that people are available to assist disputants— to listen to grievances, to represent the disputants, and to manage the process. For example, IBM has a resident manager program in which a senior manager is given the responsibility for listening to the employees in a given area, hearing their complaints and discussing what to do about them.[13]

A variant on this same idea is to hire an ombudsman. The role originated in Scandinavia to investigate the grievances of citizens against government bureaucracies. In the United States, ombudsmen deal primarily with complaints in institutions such as corporations, hospitals, prisons, and universities.[14] A central function of the ombudsman, who typically lacks decision-making power, is to be available to listen to grievances, to direct them to the appropriate person, and to see that they are dealt with expeditiously. Often the matter will be resolved if the ombudsman simply listens or provides objective information; if the complaint concerns salary, for instance, the ombudsman may provide information about average salary rates.

If disputants are unable to acquire the necessary negotiation skills, if the amount at stake is insufficient to warrant the cost of negotation skills training, or if the emotional component of the disputes is great, the designer should consider providing representatives for the disputants. In informal negotiations, a colleague might play this role; in a more formal setting a lawyer might do so.

The greater the number of parties, the greater the necessity for people who can manage the dispute resolution process. In federal rule-making negotiations, the federal agencies typically provide facilitators to bring all the parties together and orchestrate the negotiations.[15] The more complex the issues, the more technical assistance is necessary, particularly for those without technical competence or the resources to acquire it.

Mediation

One resource, a mediator who helps the disputants reach agreement, deserves separate treatment. Mediation is negotiation assisted by a third party. Negotiations often run up against roadblocks that a mediator can help remove. A mediator may be able to move the negotiations beyond name calling by encouraging the disputants to vent their emotions and acknowledge the other's perspective. A mediator can help parties move past a deadlock over positions by getting them to identify their underlying interests and develop creative solutions that satisfy those interests. Where each side is reluctant to propose a compromise out of fear of appearing weak, the mediator can make such a proposal. Mediators are thus well placed to shift the focus from rights or power to interests. Mediation can serve as a safety net to keep a dispute from escalating to a rights procedure, such as litigation, or to a power procedure, such as a strike.

Mediation is widely used in labor relations—in bargaining over contracts as well as increasingly in resolving grievances. Environmental and community mediation programs are becoming increasingly common. Mediation is used in all kinds of disputes ranging from family quarrels to business problems to international conflicts.

Peer Versus Expert Mediation. Mediation procedures come in many varieties. Perhaps the most significant factor affecting the cost of the procedure is whether the mediator is an expert from outside the organization or a peer of the disputants. Using peer mediators is not only less costly (unlike experts, they are typically unpaid) but often provides someone on the spot to intervene informally before the dispute has a chance to escalate. For example, in one San Francisco elementary school program, children are trained to mediate disputes they see brewing on the playground.[16]

One hospital in Texas provides several levels of mediation. A designer has trained large numbers of supervisors so that there is always some supervisor close to the disputants who can mediate. Key individuals in personnel, pastoral care,

and social services have also been identified as expert provid-
ers of formal mediation services. In addition, the designer has
agreed to provide professional mediators who can be called
on for assistance in particularly difficult disputes. Thus, the
hospital has three levels of mediation: informal, on-the-spot
problem-solving assistance from supervisors, experts from
within the organization, and outside professionals.[17]

Enhancing Motivation. Establishing a mediation procedure is not enough. Disputants need to be motivated to use
the procedure. The school mediation program at Bryant High
School, for instance, began with classroom seminars in conflict resolution on the assumption that students familiar with
mediation would be motivated to try it if they had a dispute.
In another sense, people who go to court are encouraged by
court officers or a judge to try mediation.[18]

Properly designed, mediation can meet some of the
same needs for emotional venting served by fighting. Particularly in those interpersonal disputes where underlying emotions are a central element, disputants can be encouraged to
express their concerns and to acknowledge the concerns of
the other side. Consider the account of a Bryant High School
girl who became involved in the school mediation program:

> All I ever wanted to do was fight. . . . I
> came into a mediation session as a disputant with
> four girls on the other side. I thought, "Who
> needs this? What am I doing here?" I just wanted
> to punch these girls out. I figured that the medi-
> ator would tell me what I was going to have to
> do. But she didn't. Instead she drew me out, lis-
> tened to me. It felt so good to let it all out: then
> I wasn't angry anymore. I thought, "Hey, if this
> can work for me, I want to learn how to do it."
> After my training, the atmosphere around me
> changed.[19]

Enhancing Skills. Mediators often need training. The
classroom seminars at Bryant High School were followed by

intensive training for mediators. The training consisted of lectures, discussion, and mock mediation in which trainees played mediators as well as parties to the dispute. The designer can use mock mediation to introduce the parties as well as potential mediators to the procedure. Disputants and mediators learn what is expected of them and see people like themselves using the procedure to work out an agreement. The grievance mediation program, for instance, provides mediation training not only for mediators but also for union and management representatives who will participate in mediation.

Providing Resources. Mediation programs require institutions to select, train, assign, and evaluate mediators. Neighborhood justice centers have been established to perform this function for community disputes. We have set up the Mediation Research and Education Project to administer grievance mediation. Such institutions can also support mediators, offering feedback on performance as well as refresher courses. They provide continuity as mediators leave and serve as a collective memory, able to evaluate the results of the program and make changes in the mediation procedure. Lastly, such institutions can serve to diffuse the program more widely within the organization or the larger community.

Risks of Mediation. In introducing a mediation procedure, the designer should be sensitive to possible unintended consequences. First, will some group, particularly susceptible to having its rights violated, likely forfeit or lose rights? For example, a corporation operating a publicly subsidized apartment building for low-income people might favor a mediation procedure to resolve tenant complaints. Such a procedure, however, could resolve complaints differently from the way they would be resolved in court. For instance, if a tenant complains about rats in her apartment, mediation might result in the landlord setting rat traps rather than engaging in the full-scale extermination program that a court would require under the city housing code. Despite this risk of forfeited rights, the designer might conclude that a mediation procedure should be made available to tenants because of its generally lower transaction costs (a matter of some concern to low-income tenants), potentially more satisfactory outcomes, and lower risk of straining the ongoing landlord-tenant relationship. In order to minimize the risk of an unknowing forfeiture of rights by tenants, the designer might include provisions for housing code education and legal counseling for tenants.[20]

A second unintended consequence is that the procedure may deter or encourage change in the distribution of power. For example, introducing a mediation program in a non-union plant may, by defusing some disputes, hinder efforts to unionize the plant. Designers considering new procedures thus should be sensitive to their impact on legal rights and the balance of power. They may want to alert the parties to such consequences and decide whether to support it.

Principle 2: Build in "Loop-Backs" to Negotiation

Interests-based procedures will not always resolve disputes, yet a rights or power contest can be excessively costly. The wise designer will thus build in procedures that encourage the disputants to turn back from such contests to negotiation. These are what we call "loop-back" procedures. It is useful to distinguish such procedures on the basis of whether they encourage disputants to "loop back" from a rights contest or from a power contest.

Looping Back from a Rights Contest

Some loop-back procedures provide information about the disputant's rights and the likely outcome of a rights contest. The disputants can then use this information to negotiate a resolution. Rights are thus determined at the lowest possible cost, while the resolution remains consensual—usually enhancing the parties' satisfaction, the quality of the relationship, and the durability of the agreement. A brief description of some of these procedures follows:

Information Procedures. In recent years, thousands of claims against asbestos manufacturers have flooded the judicial system. Some innovative designers, working as agents of the court, have set up data bases containing information about the characteristics and results of asbestos claims that have been resolved either by trial or by settlement. When a new claim is filed, the designers identify similar claims in the data base and use the information about the outcomes of previously resolved cases to determine the range within which the new case is likely to be resolved. This information reduces uncertainty about the likely outcome of the case and provides an independent standard that can help the lawyers settle the case.[21]

This procedure requires human resources: experts to design the data bank and an analytical procedure to extract information from it, experts to familiarize the lawyers with the methods, and experts to enter the data and run the analyses. The ultimate goal is to render the experts unnecessary. When a new case is filed, court clerks will be able to run a simple computer program to provide the information to the lawyers.

Advisory Arbitration. Another way to provide information about rights is advisory arbitration. While the arbitrator's decision is not binding, it provides the parties with information about the likely result if the dispute is taken to arbitration or court. This information encourages a negotiated resolution by reducing the parties' uncertainty about an adjudicated decision.

Transaction costs are typically lower than in binding arbitration or court because hearings are brief and predictions delivered orally. As a result, many courts compel the use of advisory arbitration in certain cases; they will decide only those not resolved in advisory arbitration.[22]

The grievance mediation procedure that we designed for the coal industry (described more fully in Chapter Seven) combines mediation with advisory arbitration. If mediation fails, the parties may request the third party to predict how an arbitrator would rule. Armed with this information, the parties may continue to negotiate or they may accept the predicted outcome.

Minitrials. One variant on advisory arbitration, also intended to encourage a negotiated settlement by providing information, is the minitrial. In this procedure, lawyers representing each side present evidence and arguments to representatives of the parties who have settlement authority. Ideally, these representatives are high-level executives in their own organizations who have not previously been involved in the dispute. Typically, a neutral adviser, often a former judge, is also present. After hearing the presentations, the executives try to negotiate a resolution. If they have difficulty, they may ask the neutral adviser to predict the likely outcome in court.

This procedure has several strengths. It puts negotiation in the hands of people who are not emotionally involved in the dispute and who have the perspective to view it in the context of their organizations' broad interests. It gives these people information about rights and the likely court outcome, which helps them negotiate a successful resolution.[23] It also provides lawyers with an opportunity to exercise their skills, thereby defusing their potential opposition to the procedure.

The summary jury trial is an adaptation of the minitrial, offering more direct information about likely juror reaction. The lawyers present short summaries of their cases to a mock jury selected from the court's regular jury pool. The jury deliberates and returns a verdict, typically without knowing that the verdict is only advisory. Then, as in the minitrial, representatives of the disputing parties use the information to attempt to negotiate a settlement.[24]

Looping Back from a Power Contest

The designer can also build in ways to encourage disputants to turn back from power contests and to engage in negotiations instead.

Cooling-Off Periods. Rarely does a negotiated agreement look so attractive as when the parties are on the verge of a costly power contest or are in the midst of one. One simple procedure designed to take advantage of this receptivity is a cooling-off period—a specified time during which the disputants refrain from a power contest. The Taft-Hartley Act and the Railway Labor Act both provide for cooling-off periods before strikes that threaten to cause a national emergency.[25] During the cooling-off period, negotiations, while not required, normally take place. Cooling-off periods are also useful in small-scale disputes. In the Noel Coward play *Private Lives,* a bickering couple agree that, whenever an argument threatens to get out of control, one person will shout "Solomon Isaacs," which will bring all conversation to a halt for five minutes while each tries to calm down.

Crisis Negotiation Procedures. At Caney Creek, the miners often struck without discussing their complaints with management. We recommended two additional steps to avert strikes. Before any strike, union officials would meet with management to consider the miners' concerns. The miners would then discuss management's response and vote on whether to strike.

Negotiation in times of crisis places special demands on negotiators. It may be useful therefore to provide crisis negotiation training—simulations, checklists, and standard operating procedures. It may also be helpful to establish a crisis communication mechanism. In disputes between the United States and the Soviet Union, the hotline serves this purpose. Ury has worked for the last five years with American and Soviet officials to establish "nuclear risk reduction centers"—crisis centers, staffed around the clock in Washington and Moscow, for emergency communications and negotiations aimed at preventing accidental nuclear war.[26] An agreement to set up such centers was reached in Washington on September 15, 1987, and they are now in operation.

Intervention by Third Parties. If violence breaks out during a strike or a family argument, the police intervene to stop the fighting. A form of third-party intervention is thus already built into many dispute resolution systems. In some cases, additional third-party intervention is useful. One example is the Conflict Managers Program in San Francisco schools, which trains children to intervene in playground disputes.[27] Wearing bright orange T-shirts printed with the words "Conflict Manager," the children work in pairs during lunch and recess to spot and try to mediate emerging disputes. On the international scene, neutral United Nations peace-keeping forces separate hostile forces and buy time for negotiation and mediation. Such efforts require skills training as well as such resources as administrators and third-party intervenors.

Principle 3: Provide Low-Cost Rights and Power Backups

A key part of an effective dispute resolution system is low-cost procedures for providing a final resolution based on rights or power. Such procedures serve as a backup should interests-based negotiation fail to resolve the dispute.

Low-Cost Procedures to Determine Rights

Conventional Arbitration. A less costly alternative to court is arbitration—in other words, private adjudication. Like court, arbitration is a rights procedure in which the parties (or their representatives) present evidence and arguments to a neutral third party who makes a binding decision.[28] Arbitration procedures can be simpler, quicker, and less expensive than court procedures. Formal rules need not be followed, strict time limits can be agreed to, and restrictions can be placed on the use of lawyers and of expensive evidence discovery procedures.

Arbitration has long been used to settle a variety of disputes. Today, more than 95 percent of all collective bargaining contracts provide for arbitration of disputes arising under the contract.[29] It is also used to settle some international disputes. Using the term in its broadest sense, arbitration regularly takes place in most organizations. Disputing managers will turn to a superior for a decision.[30] Within a family, children often take their disputes to parents.

Arbitration comes in several forms. Where stakes are low or similar disputes arise regularly, the parties may choose a streamlined arbitration procedure that can handle many cases quickly; this is known as expedited arbitration. Two other types of arbitration are of particular interest because they encourage the parties to loop back to negotiations: med-arb and final offer arbitration.

Med-Arb. The designer who is torn between mediation and arbitration may prescribe a hybrid, med-arb, in which the mediator serves as arbitrator if mediation fails. One advantage over mediation alone is efficiency. If mediation fails, there is no need to educate another neutral in the substance of the dispute. Another advantage is that the parties will know that the neutral will decide the dispute if they cannot, so they will pay greater attention to her suggestions, including the rights standards she may advance. A further advantage over arbitration alone is that med-arb encourages a negotiated resolution instead of an imposed one. The procedure also gives the third party the flexibility to arbitrate only those issues that the parties cannot settle themselves, so it keeps the determination of rights to a minimum and provides a built-in "loop-back" to negotiation.

Med-arb has several disadvantages. What appears to be a negotiated resolution may be perceived by the parties as an imposed one, thus diminishing the degree of satisfaction and commitment. Moreover, because the parties know that the neutral may decide the dispute, they may withhold information that would be useful in reaching a mediated settlement but that would hurt them in arbitration. Alternatively, they may reveal information to the mediator that should have no bearing on her decision if she ends up arbitrating the dispute. If the dispute must be arbitrated, it may be difficult for the mediator to discount the information and even more difficult for the losing party to believe that she did.[31]

Final-Offer Arbitration. Arbitration can encourage negotiated settlement in yet another way. In final offer arbitration, the arbitrator does not have the authority to compromise between the parties' positions but must accept one of their final offers as her decision. Each is thus under pressure to make its final offer more reasonable than the other's, anticipating that the arbitrator will adopt the more reasonable final offer as her decision. In doing so, each party will move toward the position of the other—in many cases enough so that they will be able to bridge whatever gap remains by negotiation. This procedure is most attractive when there is no well-defined rights standard for arbitral decision, so that a compromise decision is likely. It has been used successfully to bring about the negotiated resolution of disputes about the salaries of major league baseball players as well as about the terms of public-sector collective bargaining contracts.[32]

Providing Motivation, Skills, and Resources. How can one motivate parties to use arbitration if interests-based procedures have failed? If the likely alternative is court, the advantages of arbitration will supply some motivation. Still, some parties may prefer court, where an adverse decision can be far more easily appealed. Making the arbitration advisory may reassure them, especially if it is advisory for them but binding on the other side. For example, in an effort to persuade dissatisfied consumers to submit their grievances to arbitration, some business-consumer arbitration programs provide that the arbitrator's decision is binding on the business but not on the consumer.[33]

Another means of encouraging arbitration is for the parties to make a commitment in advance of any dispute to use binding arbitration. It is often easier for disputants to agree in principle to arbitration than in the context of a specific dispute. Then, when a dispute does arise, a leader can tell his constituency that his hands are tied; they are bound by contract or treaty to submit the dispute to arbitration.

If all else fails, arbitration can be made mandatory. As previously noted, some courts require disputants to submit their dispute to arbitration before they can take it to court. If negotiation fails to resolve disputes over the siting of hazardous waste facilities, the law mandates arbitration.

All these varieties of arbitration require arbitrators. The designer may need to help the parties select arbitrators. Arbitrators may need skills training; representatives of the parties may need advocacy training. Here an institution, such as the American Arbitration Association, can be helpful in providing training and arbitrators.

Low-Cost Procedures to Determine Power

Sometimes, even when interests and rights-based procedures are available, agreement is impossible because one or both parties believes it is more powerful than the other, and can obtain a more satisfactory resolution through a power contest. The designer, anticipating this situation, should consider building into the system a low-cost power procedure to be used as a backup to all other procedures. Getting the parties to accept such a procedure may be difficult, since each party is likely to oppose any new procedure that appears to give an advantage to the other. As a result, such a design effort is likely to succeed only when the use of power procedures imposes high costs on all parties. There are a variety of relatively low-cost power contests including voting, limited strikes, and rules of prudence.

Voting. Before the National Labor Relations Act (NLRA) of 1935, disputes about workers' right to engage in collective bargaining were handled through bitter strikes and violence. Some workers were killed; many were seriously injured. The NLRA did a great deal to end the violence by setting up a low-cost power contest—the union election—and by requiring employers to bargain in good faith with a union elected by a majority of the employees.

Limited Strikes. One proposal would reduce the high costs of a strike by replacing it with a mock strike. Take, for example, the 1987 professional football players' strike. Under the proposal, the employees would continue to work instead of striking—the players would continue to play football. But, as in a strike, they would forego their regular salary, and management would forego its usual profits. These sums would be placed in escrow, and a portion, gradually increasing over time, would be given to jointly selected charities. In this fashion, the power contest would continue to take place, but it would not keep the parties from pursuing their mutual goal, promoting the game of football. In the end, the power contests would be less costly to the disputants than a conventional strike because the money remaining in escrow would be returned to them when the dispute was resolved.[34]

This ingenious proposal for a lower-cost power contest has yet to be adopted, but other kinds of low-cost strikes are used occasionally. One example is the symbolic strike in which workers strike for an hour (or less) in order to demonstrate their power without incurring or inflicting high costs. In Japan, workers sometimes resort to a "stand-up" strike. Work continues as usual, but each worker wears a black armband to signal unhappiness and to keep grievances alive and visible to management.

One of our suggestions for reducing the costs of striking at Caney Creek was for the union to abandon the existing practice by which the first shift to go out on strike was the first shift to return to work, even if the dispute that led to the strike had been resolved in time for an earlier shift to return to work. The union adopted a new policy of returning to work as soon as the dispute was settled; that policy is still in effect eight years later.

As with all power contests, lower-cost contests carry the risk of unintended escalation. Skills training can sometimes help. For example, the leaders of the demonstrations at the Seabrook nuclear power plant were worried that the confrontation might turn violent, so they organized extensive training in nonviolent action for would-be protesters.[35]

Rules of Prudence. The parties may agree, tacitly or explicitly, to limit the destructiveness of tactics used in power contests. For example, youth gangs may agree to use only fists, not knives or guns in their fights. The United States and the Soviet Union observe certain rules of prudence—such as no use (explosion) of nuclear weapons, no direct use of force against the other side's troops, and no direct military action against the other's vital interests—in order to avert the highest-cost power contest, a thermonuclear war.[36]

What motivates disputants to refrain from exercising their power to its fullest extent? Almost always it is the fear that the other side will resort to similar unrestrained tactics and that both will end up incurring heavy losses. One simple rule of prudence is to stay away from the other side if contact is likely to produce a fight. That is why groups as large as nations and as small as youth gangs agree on boundaries and buffer zones.

Principle 4: Build in Consultation Before, Feedback After

A fourth design principle is to prevent unnecessary conflict and head off future disputes. This may be done through notification and consultation, as well as through post-dispute analysis and feedback.

Notification and Consultation. At Caney Creek, we recommended that management notify and consult with the union before taking action affecting employees. Notification refers simply to an announcement in advance of the intended action; consultation goes further and offers an opportunity to discuss the proposed action before it takes place. Notification and consultation can prevent disputes that arise through sheer misunderstanding. They can also reduce the anger and knee-jerk opposition that often result when decisions are made unilaterally and abruptly. Finally, they serve to identify points of difference early on so that they may be negotiated.

Post-Dispute Analysis and Feedback. Another goal is to help parties to learn from their disputes in order to prevent similar disputes in the future. Some disputes are symptomatic of a broader problem that the disputants or their organizations need to learn about and deal with. The wise designer builds into the system procedures for post-dispute analysis and feedback. At some manufacturing companies, lawyers and managers regularly analyze consumer complaints to determine what changes in product design might reduce the likelihood of similar disputes in the future. At the Massachusetts Institute of Technology, ombudsmen identify university practices that are causing disputes and suggest changes in those practices.[37]

Where a broader community interest is at stake, the designer may include a different sort of feedback: a procedure for aggregating complaints and taking action to protect the community. For example, some consumer mediation agencies keep records of complaints against each merchant and alert the appropriate state authorities when repeated complaints are lodged against the same merchant.[38]

Establishing a Forum. One means of institutionalizing consultation and post-dispute analysis is to establish a regular forum for discussion.[39] The parties may benefit from meeting regularly to discuss issues that arise in a dispute but whose causes and implications range far beyond the dispute. At Caney Creek, we revived the monthly meetings of the communications committee for this purpose. As Pacific Bell went through the wrenching transition of deregulation, the company and union formed "common interest forums" to discuss ways to work together and to prevent unnecessary disputes.[40]

Principle 5: Arrange Procedures in a Low-to-High-Cost Sequence

The design principles above suggest creating a sequence of procedures from interests-based negotiation to loop-back procedures to low-cost rights and power backups. The sequence can be imagined as a series of steps up a "dispute resolution ladder." The following is a menu of procedures to draw on in designing such a sequence:

Prevention procedures
   Notification and consultation
   Post dispute analysis and feedback
   Forum
Interests-based procedures
   Negotiation
      Quick, oral handling of disputes
      Multiple points of entry
      Established negotiation procedure
      Multiple-step negotiation
      Wise counselors
   Mediation
      Peer mediation
      Expert mediation
Loop-back procedures
   Rights
      Information procedures
      Advisory arbitration
      Minitrial
      Summary jury trial

Power
   Cooling-off periods
   Third-party intervention
Low-cost backup procedures
   Rights
      Conventional arbitration
      Expedited arbitration
      Med-arb
      Final-offer arbitration
   Power
      Voting
      Limited strikes
      Symbolic strikes
      Rules of prudence

In creating a sequence, the designer might begin with an interests-based negotiation, move to interests-based mediation, and proceed to a low-cost rights procedure. The sequence used in the oil companies' joint venture described at the beginning of this chapter contains three successive steps: first, try to catch disputes early by resolving them in the partnership committee; if that fails, bring in two uninvolved senior executives to negotiate; and, if that fails, turn to low-cost arbitration rather than to expensive litigation.

The sequence principle suggests filling potential "gaps" in the system. If parties regularly go straight from negotiation to court, the designer will want to consider intervening steps such as mediation, advisory arbitration, and arbitration. In adding steps, however, it is important to think through the possible impact of the new procedures on others already used. Adding a procedure may lead disputants to treat earlier steps as pro forma. The attractiveness and accessibility of mediation may lead disputants to negotiate less. Arranging many procedures in a sequence, each only slightly more costly than the preceding one, may have the paradoxical effect of encouraging escalation. The closer the rungs on the ladder, the easier it is to climb up. This paradox of dispute systems design ought not to stop the designer from building progressive sequences, but it should alert him to possible unintended consequences.

Principle 6: Provide the Necessary Motivation, Skills, and Resources

A final principle cuts across all others: Make sure the procedures work by providing the motivation to use them, the relevant skills, and the necessary resources. In designing a system, for example, to deal with disputes over the location of hazardous waste treatment facilities, as described earlier in the chapter, one state legislature makes negotiation mandatory and provides resources in the form of technical assistance to aid the negotiation process. Without the necessary motivation, skills, and resources, procedures might well fail.

Conclusion

This chapter has laid out six principles of dispute systems design. The first is the most central—put the focus on interests. The second is to provide rights and power procedures that loop back to negotiation. The third is to provide low-cost rights and power backups. The second and third principles thus supplement the first. The fourth design principle is to build in consultation before disputes arise and feedback after they are resolved. The fifth principle is to arrange procedures in a low-to-high-cost sequence. The final principle is to provide the motivation, skills, and resources necessary to make all these procedures work. Taken together, these six design principles constitute a practical method for cutting the costs and achieving the potential gains of conflict.

All this has been written as though the designer were the doctor and the disputants were passive patients. In fact, the parties will—and should—be active participants in all phases of the process. In the next chapter, we look at the relationship between the designer and the parties.

❖❖

Chapter 4

Making the System Work
Involving the Disputing Parties

However astute the diagnosis and ingenious the design, it is exceedingly difficult to change a dispute resolution system without working closely with the disputing parties. The designer needs their knowledge to tailor his general ideas to the particular situation. Moreover, without the parties' active support, any changes are unlikely to take hold. The process of design is as much a political task of garnering support and overcoming resistance as it is a technical task. We will discuss the process of working with the parties in four chronological phases: getting started; diagnosis and design; putting the changes into place; and exit, evaluation, and diffusion.

Getting Started

The opportunity to design a dispute resolution system most often arises in one of three circumstances: a condition of crisis has developed, an insider has come up with a "better idea," or a new relationship or organization is being established.

A Condition of Crisis

Many people do not consider changing their dispute resolution system until it has reached an acute state of distress—

disputes are costing a great deal of time and money, outcomes
are unsatisfactory, relationships are strained, and the same disputes keep recurring. Even under conditions of crisis, when
the parties invite an outsider, it is rarely to redesign the system
but rather to do something less far-reaching—put on a training program, make recommendations, or resolve a particular
dispute. The opportunity to change the system often comes
only after the designer has gained credibility and familiarity
with the parties. One designer says:

> My sense is that not a whole lot of folks
> are called in to straighten out institutions. They
> are typically called in to deal with a specific prob-
> lem. There is always somebody in power who
> doesn't see a need or doesn't want the institution
> changed. They prefer the status quo; they may be
> fearful they won't be able to adapt to change,
> that they'll be hurt by it, that they will lose con-
> trol. They like it better the way it is.[1]

The would-be designer uses the parties' dissatisfaction
with their current condition to introduce the idea of redesigning the system. This is what happened in the IBM-Fujitsu
controversy. Arbitrators were brought in to decide a large number of disputes growing out of Fujitsu's allegedly unlawful
use of IBM software. They soon realized, however, that, whatever their decision, future disputes would continue to arise.
Working with the parties, they expanded their mandate to
include designing a dispute resolution system.

A Better Idea

Not all change takes place during a crisis; some change
is incremental. At times, the power of a creative idea will be
enough to spark change. Because of the natural resistance to
calling on an outsider, such change is usually spearheaded by
insiders. Religious leaders and school administrators have
introduced mediation procedures in their institutions. Judges

have been influential in developing and promoting court-ordered arbitration, mediation, and similar changes in the judicial system.[2] Grievance mediation has been effectively introduced by both company and union insiders not because of an existing crisis but simply because it seemed like a better way to handle disputes.

A New System

The ideal time to design a dispute resolution system is at the beginning of a relationship, before disputes occur. The parties will find it easier to agree on procedures before they are embroiled in disputes whose outcomes may depend on the procedures. At the beginning, too, the designer will not have to cope with opposition from those with a stake in the existing system. Even then, however, psychological barriers exist to designing a dispute system:

> Many people find it psychologically diffi-cult to think about possible future conflict when entering into what they hope will be a harmo-nious relationship. For example, even though about one third of all marriages are likely to end in divorce, few couples (even those marrying for the second time) execute antenuptial agreements specifying how they will resolve disputes between them. In the business context, too, contracting parties are often reluctant to create a potential conflict over the terms of a dispute resolution clause in order to achieve the uncertain benefits of resolving efficiently those conflicts that may arise in the future. Another deterrent to raising the possibility of future disputes is that it may be seen as indicating a lack of commitment to the relationship.[3]

Still, some parties do foresee the likelihood of disputes and develop procedures to deal with them before they arise.

Virtually every collective bargaining contract provides procedures to deal with disputes arising under that contract. Similarly, many joint venture agreements between corporations
contain carefully drafted dispute resolution clauses.[4] Nations,
too, occasionally make advance provision for the resolution
of disputes. For example, the SALT I treaty between the
United States and the Soviet Union provides for the establishment of a Standing Consultative Commission, which seeks to
resolve disputes over perceived violations of the treaty.[5]

The lesson for the designer is clear: when parties are
entering a relationship in which disputes are likely, he should
urge them to design a low-cost dispute resolution system
before disputes arise, not after.

Gaining Acceptance

Whichever way the designer becomes involved—crisis,
better idea, or new system—his first problem is gaining acceptance by all parties. Where the designer is already associated
with one party, a perception of bias may result. In that situation, the designer may want to identify an ally on the other
side with whom he can work, so as to counter the perception
of bias. If the designer is an outsider invited in by one side, he
may want to consult with the other side about a joint invitation. Making almost simultaneous contact with all parties
can be critical; if one party in a conflict situation believes
that the designer has become closer to the other, the designer's
credibility may be jeopardized.

From the time of first contact with the parties, the
designer needs to be especially sensitive, just as a mediator
would, to hidden agendas and the conflicts between and
within the parties. At Caney Creek, for example, we discovered that we had been invited in by one faction of management that hoped that we would lend support to their views
and help them prevail over an opposing faction in the internal management debate about how to deal with the conflict.

The designer who is invited has an easier time being
accepted than one who is imposed or who takes the initiative,

but an invitation is no guarantee of acceptance. Invitations by leaders on both sides may provide only token participation on the part of constituents or subordinates. At Caney Creek, although we were invited by senior union and company officials, we soon discovered that we had been imposed on the local union and local management officials. Still later, we realized that gaining acceptance from the local union leadership was not tantamount to gaining acceptance from the membership.

Involving the Parties in Diagnosis and Design

To gather information and support from all parties, the designer should involve them from the outset in the process of diagnosis and design. If the parties are not involved in the process, they are less likely to approve the product, no matter how good it is from an objective point of view.

Several different approaches are available for involving the parties in diagnosis and design: establishing a design committee, engaging in shuttle mediation, and persuading key decision makers or opinion leaders.[6]

Establishing a Design Committee

After identifying all relevant parties, the designer may invite them to select representatives for a committee to help diagnose and design the system. The design committee often serves as a liaison between the designer and the parties. One designer told us:

> We use people who represent different interest groups to help us design a process, give us feedback, keep us on track, and provide a bridge between the designer and the disputing parties. The design committee negotiates out the procedure and then it's not the designer who sells it, it's this group that sells it. If somebody disagrees, a committee member from their side can

say, "Well, wait a minute, this is why we did it
this way." This process creates greater ownership
of the process and a higher commitment to joint
problem-solving.[7]

As another designer put it, each member of the design
committee serves as a "quasi mediator" between the constituency she represents and the other side.[8] Each actively consults
with her constituency to ensure that agreed-upon procedural
changes will have the support of the eventual users.[9]

Engaging in Shuttle Mediation

When hostility and distrust between the parties threaten
to render joint sessions unproductive, shuttle mediation may
succeed in engaging the parties. In this process, the designer
meets with the parties separately, moving back and forth
between them, trying out ideas about changes in the dispute
resolution system until either an agreement is reached or the
level of hostility diminishes sufficiently that joint meetings
can be held. This is a process we used at Caney Creek.
One aid to shuttle mediation is the "one-text" procedure. With this procedure, the designer begins with a single
draft containing his own ideas as well as those contributed by
the parties. The designer presents the draft not as his formal
recommendation but simply as some rough ideas culled from
the parties' suggestions and the designer's experience. He does
not ask the parties to accept or reject the ideas at this point
but simply to criticize: Where do these ideas fail to address
the problem of high disputing costs? What would stand in
the way of the procedures being used? How could the ideas be
improved? What else is needed?[10]
After consultation with the parties, the designer edits
and revises the draft, trying to incorporate changes suggested
by one side without making the proposed system worse for
the other. Then he returns to the parties, again for constructive criticism rather than acceptance or rejection. He goes
back to work on the program of changes, and reemerges to

ask for yet further criticism. Finally—perhaps after three rounds, perhaps after twenty-three—he has a design that carries the imprint of all those who offered criticism. Only at that point, after he has done his best to satisfy the parties' concerns, does he submit the design for their formal approval.

Focusing on Key Actors

In some situations, the designer may need the support of key actors with control over the system even more than he needs the support of actual disputants. One example is the process that led to the establishment of the so-called multidoor courthouse in the District of Columbia:[11]

> The original instigator was . . . the founder and director of the Citizens Complaint Center. . . . She brought the idea to the Presiding Judge of the Family Division of the Superior Court, because she saw that getting a key judge involved was important and thought perhaps installation of the multidoor courthouse notion in the domestic relations context was the way to go. However, the Family Division Presiding Judge saw the possibility of a more multifaceted initiative and took it to the Chief Judge of the Superior Court. The Chief Judge in turn convened the D.C. Corporation Counsel, bar leaders, business leaders, and representatives of the City Council and the U.S. Attorney's Office, so that most of the major actors in the system had a stake in the idea from the outset.[12]

Another example of focusing on key actors is our establishment of grievance mediation in the coal industry. We began by securing the approval in principle of the presidents of the union and the coal operators' association. Next we dealt with union district presidents and company labor relations directors. They, too, approved the procedure in principle but told us that the procedure, even if adopted, would rarely be used unless we could convince local union officers and mine labor relations directors of its merits. Conversely, we were told that if local union and management leaders supported the procedure, individual disputants—miners and their supervisors—would at least try it. Consequently, we worked hard at selling the procedure to local leaders. As predicted, where local leadership was enthusiastic, the procedure got off to a good start; elsewhere, use was sparse.

The designer is well-advised to focus on key actors where they strongly influence the procedures used by actual disputants. Even in such situations, however, the designer may need to canvass potential users of the system so as to better understand what might motivate them to use new procedures.[13]

The Designer's Balancing Act

If the designer is to get the parties to agree to try a new dispute resolution system, he must be adept at balancing three quite separate roles: expert, mediator, and negotiator. He will wear his expert's hat when analyzing the current system and formulating potential design alternatives, his mediator's hat when working with the disputing parties to construct a system that meets their concerns, and his negotiator's hat when selling design ideas to them. One designer describes how he switches hats while designing a system for a prison:

> I negotiate with the parties to get our [design team's] ideas on the table so we have a framework. Then I can relax a little bit, negotiating only to keep people from undoing the design or doing something terrible. But then you have to go to the administrator to make sure he or she understands what's been done and accepts things thus far. Otherwise you work for two or three months, deliver this wonderful package, and the administrator says, "I can't do this," and

you've got to take the message back. So there is
this mediating between the design committee and
the administrator and also negotiating directly
with them.[14]

Dealing with Opposition

Even if all parties are involved in the change process,
some individuals or groups may actively oppose the new
procedures. Some may perceive threats to their roles as administrators or advocates in the existing dispute system. Others
may believe that they have been "winning" disputes with
existing procedures and that any change would be to their
disadvantage.

Dealing with Those Whose Role Is Threatened. Probation officers may oppose a plan to send all juvenile first
offenders to a community justice procedure instead of a juvenile court, in part because reducing the number of juveniles
who require supervision could decrease the need for probation
officers. Labor arbitrators may oppose grievance mediation
because it may reduce the number of grievances going to
arbitration. Lawyers may oppose court-sponsored arbitration
procedures that may result in fewer trials. Sometimes dis-
guised, sometimes overt, the fear of losing work can be powerful. The most effective approach when dealing with this
kind of fear is to show opponents that they can play a role in
the new procedure. Lawyers have been attracted to the minitrial and the summary jury trial described in Chapter Three,
because in those procedures they perform their traditional
function of presenting evidence and argument to a decision
maker. Similarly, we have pointed out to worried labor arbitrators that their knowledge and experience of industrial relations and the interpretation of collective bargaining contracts
make them well suited to serve as mediators in a grievance
mediation procedure.

Sometimes a new procedure will inevitably diminish
the role of individuals or groups that were important in prior
procedures, and no equivalent role can be designed for them

in the new procedure. In such cases, the designer must prepare the parties to expect their opposition and work with supporters of change in planning how to deal with it.

Dealing with Those Who Believe They Have Been "Winning." Why should teachers participate in the design of a procedure that will make it easier for students to raise complaints about their grades? Why should a government agency that has been successful in defending itself against legal claims participate in designing a procedure for reconciling interests rather than determining rights? Understandably, parties who are "winning" with the current system may be unwilling to help change it.

The designer has several available approaches. He might point out that if the winning parties fail to participate in the change process, the new system may ignore their interests. He may also show them that, even if they "win" fewer disputes under the new system, they may be better off overall as a result of reduced transaction costs, less recurrence of disputes, and a better ongoing relationship. This is the point that we make to companies or unions that oppose grievance mediation because in the past they have won a majority of arbitrated grievances. A designer might make the same point to the president of a manufacturing concern that wins most of its lawsuits with its distributors but loses many distributors in the process.

To the extent that opposition rests on unfounded or exaggerated fears, it may be diminished by making changes experimentally. A demonstration can be arranged in one site or for a limited period of time. For example, we encourage disputing parties to experiment with grievance mediation for six months or ten grievances. Opposition based on fear of the unknown typically subsides sufficiently to allow the procedure to be given a short-term trial run.[15]

Putting the Changes into Place

It is a long way from the drawing board to the construction site. New interests are inevitably uncovered as parties who signed off on new procedures nevertheless resist using them. Some parties' reluctance stems from fear that they lack or cannot learn necessary skills. Details of the design that are impossible to specify beforehand may generate obstacles that have a direct bearing on the effectiveness of the total changes. It is unlikely that any system will work without adjustment, whether in procedures, motivations, skills, or resources.

One designer describes the early days of trying to implement a program to mediate interpersonal disputes in a neighborhood:

> We just started out and got a group of about twenty-five people to go through the first round of [mediation] training. We did a couple of [mediation sessions], didn't like what [the mediators] did, asked that they be retrained, trained them again, and saw some more [sessions]. It felt like, "We have to do better than that," so we trained them again and kept changing the training program based on the [mediation] experience. After about a year and a half of that, we realized we had something.[16]

Putting the changes into place involves two tasks: motivating the parties to use the new procedures and helping them develop the skills to do so.

Motivating the Disputants to Use New Procedures

Much of the work of diagnosis and design consists of making new procedures attractive to disputants. Even if the procedures are appealing on paper, disputants may be reluctant to use them. The designer may be able to overcome this reluctance in several ways: by demonstrating the procedures, using leaders as examples, using peers as proponents, setting goals, providing incentives, and publicizing early successes.

Demonstrating the Procedures. In order to overcome
potential users' skepticism about a new procedure, the
designer can encourage them to talk to others who have been
using a similar procedure. Even better, they can be invited to
observe that procedure in action. Or, if those experienced
with the procedure are not easily accessible, new users can try
it out in a simulation. Following such a simulation, one
participant said:

> You know, I think I'm going to be able to
> work with this person. I found out that she was
> willing to disclose information and willing to
> consider my interests in the simulation. If she's
> willing to do that in real life, we've got a capacity
> to work together.[17]

Using Leaders as Examples. Leaders can also act as role
models to encourage parties to adopt a change. At Caney
Creek, we recommended that the mine superintendent spend
time underground with the miners, talking with them and
listening to their grievances. Our aim was to set an example
for the foremen—if they saw their boss engaged in negotiation, they might try it too. A leader's approach to grievances
sends a strong signal to others in the organization about the
appropriate and rewarding way to resolve disputes.

Using Peers as Proponents. People who have been
involved in designing or using a new procedure are often best
at selling it to others. A designer working in a prison asked
design committee members to explain the new procedures to
the inmates. She says, "When a high status inmate representative goes around and talks about a procedure he has been
part of putting together, the others think then maybe it's
worth trying."[18] Likewise, students trained as mediators for
school disputes encourage their friends to try mediation, and
lawyers trained as divorce mediators encourage their clients
to consider mediation.[19]

Setting Goals. One of the most successful motivation
techniques is getting the parties to set specific, challenging

goals.[20] At International Harvester, the goal was simple: settle all grievances orally on the day they arise. Previous exhortations such as "settle grievances as quickly as possible" had been difficult to enforce because they were vague. No clear yardstick existed against which progress could be measured. With the help of a clear goal, however, the results were dramatic—virtually all grievances were being resolved orally.[21]

Designing Incentives. To ensure that new procedures are used, the designer may provide for special rewards. He may, for instance, seek to make dispute resolution part of each manager's performance appraisal or make the acquisition of dispute resolution skills part of managers' annual development plans.

Publicizing Early Successes. Publicizing early successes of the new dispute resolution system gives momentum to the change process. At International Harvester, for example, a spotlight was put on success stories:

> Certain ceremonial gestures helped people to identify with the new program. Top officials complimented the local people for their hard work and for their willingness to make a change. A sense of momentum was also created by talking about the success which the program was achieving in other situations. Finally, pictures were taken and people's comments printed in a company magazine. All of these devices created an aura of good feeling about the "new look."[22]

The Designer's Presence. The impact of the designer's presence during implementation should not be overlooked. It can signal to all involved that a major change is under way. The designer serves as a symbol of and a watchdog over the new procedural norms. Without him, it is all too easy for people to fall back into the old familiar routines, particularly under the pressures of immediate crises and deep-seated conflicts. The designer who is present reminds the parties to use lower-cost interests-based procedures whenever possible.

Training and Coaching Disputants

One of the designer's most important implementation tasks is helping the disputants acquire the skills to use the new procedures effectively. Since new procedures will most often be interests-based, this typically means training and coaching in negotiation and mediation skills.

Training. Successful training programs combine presentation, demonstration, and discussion of appropriate techniques with simulation exercises and feedback.[23] Training the parties together is valuable. Joint training gives participants a common vocabulary with which to discuss alternative approaches to resolving disputes; it instills common expectations about appropriate behavior in interests-based negotiation and provides a safe environment in which to try out new procedures. It also offers an opportunity to jointly set goals for using the new procedures.

The designer must decide whom to train and how intensely. Training large numbers of potential disputants can help, even if the training is brief. In the mediation project at Bryant High School, more than 3,000 students attended classroom seminars on mediation and nonviolent problem solving. As a result, almost any time a dispute arose, several students were present who knew how to use a problem-solving approach to resolve it.[24] Even some parties who seem personally unsuited for interests-based negotiation may benefit from training. Consider the story of "Heavy" told by one designer:

> The first prison we worked in in New York was a big maximum security place, a couple of thousand men locked up. And one of the men on the design committee who later became a committee member was a guy named Heavy. I don't remember what his first name was but they called him Heavy because he just sat there. I don't know how smart Heavy was, he was just a moose of a guy who apparently had a very quick temper, which we saw a little bit of, and who also in his earlier days had been very quick with his fists.

> When we got this thing going, Heavy got the training. Sometime after it started, a grievance clerk said, "I can't believe it. Yesterday Heavy got into an argument and I thought he was going to drop the sucker right in his tracks. Heavy just kept talking to him!" I don't know how much of this you can attribute to the training, but the guy who was talking to us was attributing all of it to the fact that Heavy had learned that he didn't have to drop people in their tracks, he could talk to them and get something out of that.[25]

The designer will also want to provide continuity by establishing an ongoing program for familiarizing and training new people to participate in the new procedures. Both school and neighborhood mediation programs have been successful in sustaining their dispute resolution procedures despite the turnover of mediators. They have done this primarily by periodically training large numbers of mediators so that newly trained people can work side by side with more experienced mediators.

Coaching. Ideally, the designer will coach the disputants through their initial disputes. He will encourage each participant to prepare by identifying interests, creating options, and considering trade-offs. After the negotiations, the designer can debrief participants and give them feedback on their process skills. Such coaching can be provided in person or by telephone.[26] Two risks are associated with coaching: creating the appearance of bias and succumbing to the temptation to mediate. These risks can be minimized if the designer makes his services available to all parties and avoids providing advice on the substantive aspects of the dispute.

Exit, Evaluation, and Diffusion

Exit

The parties may become dependent on the designer for coaching, motivation to use new procedures, and adjustments to the design. The designer serves as a temporary support in the construction of the system. At some point, however, he must leave and the new structure has to be able to stand by itself. The designer must therefore balance the benefits of managing the implementation against the risks of continuing the parties' reliance on him. At Caney Creek, Ury sometimes had difficulty remembering that he was not there to mediate but to support the parties in implementing a new dispute resolution system. The key is to give the changes a chance. Occasionally, this will mean lending the parties a helping hand. More often, it will mean letting them stumble and learn for themselves.

Evaluation

The purpose of evaluation is to determine whether the changes are working as intended.[27] Are the costs of disputing reduced? Are the benefits being realized? Are there unintended consequences? Evaluation helps the designer fine tune the changes. Moreover, if a designer intends to disseminate the new procedures, it is critical that he learn as much as possible from the initial experiments.

Evaluation focuses on three questions:

1. *Does the new system work?* Are transaction costs lower? Are parties more satisfied with outcomes? Has the quality of the relationship improved? Has recurrence of disputes been reduced? In other words, what changes has the new system brought about? The evaluator also looks for negative side effects of the intervention, both anticipated and unanticipated.

2. *What are the limits on the effectiveness of the changes?* In other words, under what specific conditions will they work? For example, in designing the grievance mediation program we assumed that even experienced mediators would need substantial arbitration experience in order to be successful. Evaluation, however, revealed that mediators with little arbitration experience were as successful as experienced arbitrators.

3. *Why do the changes work?* What are the most important factors that make for success? It may be that the new system succeeds for wholly different reasons than those that the designer imagined. These surprises help the designer to revise his working theory and improve future efforts. In evaluating our grievance mediation program we unexpectedly found that the reduction in transaction costs was most important to unions, while a perceived improvement in the parties' relationship was most important to employers. As a result, in our efforts to spread grievance mediation, we have emphasized the former to unions and the latter to employers.

Who Should Evaluate? Evaluation should take place as the program proceeds. While the designer is familiar with the project and knows better than anyone else what he is trying to accomplish, he may be biased toward finding improvement. Hiring an outside evaluator will reduce the risk of bias. It may, however, increase costs substantially because the evaluator will have to duplicate much of the diagnosis done by the designer.

Whether the evaluation is directed by the designer or by an outsider, the parties should actively participate. They can best identify positive and negative consequences of the change. Eliciting their assistance will also promote their capacity for self-evaluation and help them spot problems early. If the parties learn to recognize when procedures are not working, they may be able to continue the process of improving the system themselves, eventually rendering the designer obsolete.

How Detailed an Evaluation? Evaluation takes time and costs money, but if the designer has any intention of trying to extend the program elsewhere, he will find solid evaluation data valuable in responding to skeptics at new sites. Such data have been central to our efforts to spread grievance mediation. We could talk indefinitely about the capacity of mediation to resolve disputes, but nothing is more convincing than the record of settling 850 of the first 1,000 disputes.

Diffusion (an Optional Step)

The most common form of diffusion is replication— the transfer of a procedure from one site to another.[28] This method is essentially horizontal—across major organizational lines. We have used this strategy for the diffusion of grievance mediation. Goldberg has made numerous presentations on grievance mediation at conferences, written articles for institutional newsletters, and followed up with countless face-to-face meetings to explain the process to particular unions and companies. A simpler and less time-consuming alternative is to spread change vertically within an organization or industry. A decision at the top of a company can extend new procedures from a single plant to an entire corporation. A multiemployer collective bargaining agreement can extend changes from a single corporation to an entire industry.

Government action can also encourage diffusion. To stimulate the use of court-ordered arbitration, some states have adopted legislation authorizing arbitration programs, and Congress has appropriated funds for pilot programs in the federal courts. Congress also has directed states to provide an ombudsman program for senior citizens residing in long-term care facilities.[29]

However diffusion takes place, the designer must always consider whether a procedure that was designed for a particular relationship, community, or institution will transfer successfully to a new location. A procedure that works in one location may not work in another, unless it is supported by motivations, skills, and resources similar to those present at the original site. Moreover, broader environmental conditions may differ: a procedure that works in one culture may not work in another. Rights procedures may be less successful in a culture that places a premium on accommodation, and interests-based procedures may be less successful in a culture with a strong orientation toward right and wrong.

Conclusion

In working with the parties, the dispute systems designer plays the roles of coach, evaluator, and evangelist, in addition to those of expert, mediator, and negotiator. He acts as an expert when he analyzes the current system and considers potential alternatives. Acting as a mediator, he seeks to bring about agreement on changes to the system. In doing so, he also negotiates with the parties to adopt the changes he thinks worthwhile. In helping the parties begin to use the new system, he becomes a coach, working to develop their skills, and sustaining their enthusiasm when agreements cannot be reached. He may also evaluate the system, helping the parties determine how well it is working and what adjustments should be made. If he takes on the task of diffusion, the designer plays yet another role, that of evangelist. In the case study that follows, we played all these roles.

❖❖❖

Part Two

Building Dispute Systems

Cases from the Coal Industry

In the next three chapters, we describe the experiences in the coal industry that provided the basis for our framework of dispute systems design. Chapter Five recounts our diagnosis of the wildcat strikes that plagued the coal industry in the 1970s. Chapter Six discusses our intervention at strike-ridden Caney Creek mine, where we acted for the first time as systems designers—carrying out a dispute resolution diagnosis, designing a less costly system, and helping the parties implement the agreed upon changes. In Chapter Seven, we return to the industry level, describing our efforts to mediate grievances in the coal industry and elsewhere by designing and implementing an interests-based procedure.

In reading these chapters, it is important to remember that when we did the work described, we were learning as we went along. As a result, the reader will notice (as we have) a number of instances in which our hindsight is considerably better than was our foresight. We have made no effort to rewrite history to make ourselves appear wiser than we actually were. We believe it will be more useful for readers to learn as we did from our mistakes. Thus, we encourage readers to ask repeatedly: Why did they do that? What result were they trying to achieve? Is there a better way to achieve that result?

❖❖

Chapter 5

Diagnosing an Industry's Problems

Wildcat Strikes in the Coal Mines

In November 1973, Red Arrow Mine was shut down by a wildcat strike—the sixth in as many months.[1] Although the reason for the strike was unclear, the miners had been complaining about the lack of hot water in the bathhouse where they showered after work. The superintendent's reaction to the strike was immediate. He discharged the miner suspected of instigating the strike and notified the union that discussions about hot water in the bathhouse were suspended until the strike ended. The miners responded that they would not return to work until the discharged miner had been reinstated. To put pressure on the company, they sent pickets to shut down other mines owned by the same company.[2] Striking and picketing continued for three days, until the company convinced a federal judge to order the miners back to work.[3] The miners reluctantly complied. Six months later, an arbitrator denied the discharged miner's grievance, seeking reinstatement, and the miners struck again in protest.

Although Red Arrow is a fictitious mine, this sequence of events—complaint, unsuccessful negotiations, strike, discharge, picketing, court injunction to return to work, arbitrator's decision against the miner, another strike—was played out time and time again across the coal fields in the early and mid 1970s. In the period from 1971 to 1974, there were an average of 1,500 strikes per year. The rate doubled from 1975 to 1977 to more than 3,000 strikes per year.[4] No one seemed to know what to do about the strikes. In fact, no one seemed to understand why the miners were resorting to striking when they had a grievance procedure culminating in arbitration. This chapter describes our research on wildcat strikes, which, as it turned out, was the first step in our becoming dispute systems designers. The findings of the wildcat strike study provided the foundation for many of our recommendations at Caney Creek, as well as our introduction of mediation into the coal industry's grievance procedure.

At the time we began, though, we were not self-consciously acting as systems designers. Our focus was research, and our study was intended to investigate causes, not evaluate potential solutions. We intended to do what we had done in our previous work: conduct empirical research leading to recommendations that interpreted the findings for practitioners.[5] We did not intend to use the findings to campaign for change in the coal industry's labor-management practices.

Entry: Negotiating Funding and Access

We began to work on the problems of access to data and funding in a series of trips to Washington, D.C., in the spring of 1976. We met first with Arnold Miller, president of the United Mine Workers of America, and Joseph P. Brennan, president of the Bituminous Coal Operators' Association (BCOA, the employers' association with which the union negotiates its collective bargaining agreement).[6]

From Brennan, we wanted data from the association's files on wildcat strikes in the industry and a statement of support for the study to help us in seeking funding. He agreed to both requests. Our meeting with Arnold Miller was also cordial. We had been concerned that he might believe that the study would interfere with the miners' use of the wildcat strike as a tactic in dealing with management. We decided to confront his potential opposition directly. We told him that our research was intended to identify the conditions that cause wildcat strikes, and that if these conditions could be eliminated, the need for strikes might decline. Miller accepted this explanation and wrote a letter of support that we could use in seeking funding and in attempting to persuade local union leaders to participate.

Our negotiations with funding agencies were not nearly so successful. Despite the energy crisis of the early 1970s and the federal energy policy to increase the use of coal, none of the various agencies involved in implementing this policy was willing to fund our research on wildcat strikes. We did receive financial support from the National Science Foundation.

Diagnosis

The Conflict Environment

We knew that miners in many countries were strike-prone[7] and that the UMWA had a long-standing tradition of wildcat strikes. Still, we were puzzled about the causes of the current wave of strikes. After all, the miners' contract provided for final and binding arbitration, which was intended to eliminate the need to strike.

One explanation for the high strike rate of the mid 1970s undoubtedly lay in the bitter struggle for control of the UMWA, which culminated in the 1972 election of Arnold Miller to the union presidency. Under Miller, the UMWA embarked on a program of decentralization of authority and democratization that combined with continuing internal political conflict, produced weak union leadership. Thus, there were few restraints from within the union on wildcat strikes led by the rank and file. Each side blamed the other for the strikes. Management insisted that the union increase its discipline over members; union officials and miners said that the fault lay with management, which engaged in practices that violated the contract; the solution was to eliminate those practices.

Another possibility was that the miners struck because they believed the overloaded grievance arbitration procedure was not effective in protecting their contractual rights. A 1972 study attributed the strike problem to excessive delay in the grievance arbitration system.[8] But this answer seemed too simplistic. The overloaded system was slow, but no slower than more lightly used systems in other industries not plagued by wildcat strikes.

Establishing Local Differences in Strike Frequency

The first key to unraveling the wildcat strike problem, we concluded, was to determine whether strike frequency differed among mines.[9] If there were differences, then we would try to identify their causes. (Technically, our study was designed to identify correlates, not causes.) We hoped that once the factors associated with strikes were identified, at least some of them would prove susceptible to change. We began by collecting data about strike frequency in 1975 and 1976 at 293 underground mines in West Virginia, Virginia, Kentucky, Tennessee, Ohio, Indiana, Illinois, and Pennsylvania.[10] We were looking for statistically significant differences in strike frequency between companies, between union districts, and between mines operated by the same company. We found them. For example, in 1975 one company had eleven mines with no strikes, two mines with eleven strikes, and one mine with sixteen strikes.

The Conflict Environment at High- and Low-Strike Mines

We then investigated the conflict environment at the high- and low-strike mines. One theory held that strikes reflected the miners' frustration with unsatisfactory living or working conditions. We found no support for this view. High-strike mines were not located predominantly in the more remote areas of Appalachia, where the quality of life was particularly poor. Nor were they predominantly mines where productivity was especially high or safety standards low.[11] Nor did they differ from low-strike mines in terms of underground conditions (gassy, wet, low roofs).

Dispute Resolution at the Mine Site

Our next step was to select four mines operated by two different companies but all in the same union district.[12] From each company we chose one mine with frequent strikes and one mine where strikes were rare. At each mine, we interviewed the mine superintendent, the mine manager, the company personnel or labor relations coordinator, all local union officers, and about thirty randomly selected miners.[13] Our goal was to find out whether the parties were using different procedures for resolving disputes at low-strike mines than at high-strike mines and whether they differed with respect to motivations, skills, and resources to use various procedures.

The Dispute Resolution System in the Coal Industry. The bituminous coal contract provides for a four-step grievance procedure (a prescribed dispute resolution system with four procedures). At step 1, the miner with a grievance presents his claim to his immediate foreman, who has twenty-four hours to respond. If the miner is not satisfied with the foreman's response, he may proceed to step 2 and ask the mine committee to discuss the grievance with the mine manager or the superintendent. The grievant and the foreman usually attend this meeting, which must take place within five working days of the foreman's decision. If the mine committee and management do not reach agreement, the grievance may go to step 3, a meeting between a district-level union field representative (each miner belongs to a local; a group of locals in the same geographical area constitutes a district) and a representative of the employer (frequently someone who is not based at the mine site). This meeting must take place within seven working days of a request. If agreement is not reached, the union may take the grievance to step 4, arbitration, where it is heard by a third party who makes a final and binding decision.

Despite this standardized procedure, we found that disputes were resolved differently at high- and low-strike mines. The differences included the level at which final resolution occurred, the approach taken to negotiation, the attention given to prevention, and the availability of "loop-back" procedures.

Resolution at as Low a Level as Possible. Step 1 of the grievance procedure requires a miner to raise his complaint with his foreman. According to the miners at the low-strike mines, foremen were resolving many complaints. At the high-strike mines, they were not.

An Interests Approach to Dispute Resolution. Step 2 of the grievance procedure is a negotiation between the union mine committee and the mine manager or superintendent. At high-strike mines, the step was often pro forma. As the superintendent at one high-strike mine described his approach, "80 to 90 percent of the grievances have no contractual basis. I tell the mine committee to write it up and send it to step 3." A mine committee member confirmed this approach, saying, "every time, they say 'well, we'll send it up to arbitration.' They don't want to settle at the mines where we're supposed to." At high-strike mines, interests-based complaints were being transformed into rights-based grievances because local management was unwilling to deal with interests directly. If a complaint was not based on rights reflected in the UMWA-BCOA contract, management would not consider it. Management at low-strike mines used an entirely different approach. The story of the stolen boots (Chapter One) was told to us by the superintendent at one of the low-strike mines. Although the miner had no contractual right to new boots, the superintendent had bought boots for miners in the past when it had been in the company's interest to do so, and he would have done so in this case. In telling this story, the superintendent implied that the shift boss's strict rights approach to resolving the dispute had been a contributing factor in the wildcat strike.

Dispute Prevention. Superintendents at the low-strike mines used a variety of techniques to prevent disputes. They met regularly with the mine communications committee to announce and discuss proposed management actions that would affect the miners. At the high-strike mines, in contrast, meetings between superintendents and committees were irregular and pro forma. The superintendents at the low-strike mines also spent a considerable amount of time underground.

There they were not only accessible to miners but willing to talk with them about complaints. At high-strike mines, upper management rarely ventured underground.

"Loop-Back" Procedures. Another characteristic of low-strike mines was the practice of adding informal settlement procedures to the formal grievance procedure in order to encourage negotiations. At one low-strike mine, the manager had the personnel coordinator investigate all grievances before the step 2 meeting. This mine manager used the information provided by the personnel coordinator to help him judge the reasonableness of both the union's claim and lower-level management's rejection of that claim. According to him, this information kept the step 2 meeting from turning into a whom-do-you-believe contest. At the other low-strike mine, any grievance not settled at step 2 led to another meeting between the grievant, the mine committee, and the superintendent, as well as his superior (who did not attend step 2 meetings).

Rights Contests: The Miners' Experiences with Arbitration

Not surprisingly, the high-strike mines were sending more of their grievances to step 3 and arbitration than the low-strike mines were. Miners everywhere lacked confidence in the arbitration procedure. They complained about the slowness of the process and about the decisions themselves. One miner explained his lack of confidence in arbitrators by telling this story: "The men couldn't get transportation inside the mine and grieved, and the arbitrator went against the men and later we found out that the arbitrator didn't even know what a 'mantrip' [a vehicle for conveying miners into the mine] was. Most arbitrators never even seen the inside of a mine." Further diminishing the miners' confidence in the arbitrators was the fact that approximately 40 percent of those arbitrators' decisions that were reviewed by the Arbitration Review Board were revised or modified.[14] Competence, moreover, was not the only problem. A majority of the miners at each mine thought that they lost some grievances because the arbitrators were biased or unfair. Two-thirds of the miners we interviewed believed that the arbitrators were taking bribes from the companies.

Power Contests: The Motivation for Striking

Miners' perceptions of the utility of striking differed dramatically. Twenty-eight percent of the miners at the high-strike mines believed that striking was necessary to get management to talk about their problems; only 3 percent of miners at the low-strike mines held that view. Miners at the high-strike mines, but not at the low-strike mines, also believed that striking helped to resolve disputes in their favor. Large proportions of miners at both high- and low-strike mines told us that few strikes concerned issues that were worth striking for. The miners participated in the strikes because of the union tradition of solidarity—helping a fellow union member in his battle with management today assured his help in your battle tomorrow—and partly because of fear of reprisals from other union members if they did not participate.

Some of our preconceptions proved erroneous. We had thought that management's disciplinary actions against strikers might discourage striking, but we found that miners did not fear disciplinary procedures at either high- or low-strike mines. The company's most severe disciplinary weapon, discharge, rarely posed a serious threat. Many arbitrators would reverse a discharge for striking unless management could prove that the discharged miner had instigated the strike, and management had difficulty coming up with such proof. We had also thought that union disciplinary procedures might discourage striking. It was possible that local union leadership was more powerful at low-strike mines and that it used that power to discourage striking. We found, however, that though all local presidents attempted to dissuade miners from striking, none used internal union disciplinary procedures to do so.[15] One local president at a low-strike mine explained, "The men is the local. Just because I'm president, that don't give me no power over them. I can't tell them what to do."

The Costs of Disputing

Though we did no formal analysis of transaction costs, the resources consumed by the strikes were undoubtedly great. For the miners, the costs were lost wages and fringe benefits. For the companies, the costs were continuing salaries paid to supervisory personnel and overhead charges. For miners and companies, a long-term cost was the loss of sales contracts to more reliable sources, particularly nonunion mines.

As might be expected, the relationship between union and management at the high-strike mines was poor. Mine committee members reported that management was uncooperative; that it refused to settle a dispute even when the union had a good claim. Similarly, management reported that the mine committee was uncooperative and that it abused its power. Such reports were substantially less frequent at the low-strike mines. The parties' attitudes toward each other are a product of previous negotiations and strikes. Although unfavorable attitudes probably do not directly cause strikes, they do affect perceptions and expectations about negotiations. At high-strike mines, management and union leaders expect adversarial negotiations and develop appropriate strategies. Over time, the parties' expectations of conflict develop a life of their own, which acts as a barrier to any change in the quality of the relationship.

Implications of the Diagnosis

Our most important finding was that it was possible to operate a coal mine under a UMWA contract without frequent wildcat strikes. But to do so, we found, takes a significant amount of skill and effort on the part of both local union and management officials. Both parties need to try to negotiate a settlement at step 2. When step 2 is pro forma, miners are denied a voice in the resolution of their disputes, and the probability that they will be dissatisfied with the outcome increases. In step 2 negotiations, both parties also need to avoid focusing exclusively on rights and be willing to search jointly for interests-based resolutions.

Miners everywhere preferred resolving grievances without resort to arbitration. Although many grievances were being arbitrated, especially at high-strike mines, miners lacked confidence in the arbitration procedure. It put them in the position of being a passive spectator, watching a representative argue the contractual merits of their grievance. Furthermore, they did not expect a satisfactory outcome from arbitration. Striking, in contrast, offered emotional release and revenge, and it sometimes forced reluctant mine management to negotiate—that is, it provided miners with some voice and some satisfactory outcomes, both of which were denied at step 2 and arbitration.

Design: Recommendations for Change

The question then became how to turn a high-strike relationship into a low-strike one. We made a number of recommendations, little thinking that one day we would have the opportunity to put our ideas into practice at Caney Creek. In making these recommendations, we had forsaken the role of the pure social scientist who collects, analyzes, and publishes data for others to interpret. We did so because we realized that regardless of whether we developed the implications of the data, others would. We knew the study and the data better than anyone else, so we concluded that we should make recommendations. Still, we were not thinking of ourselves as systems designers. We took no steps to persuade the parties to accept our recommendations for change. Nor did we propose that we would play a role in implementing any changes that were accepted.

Dispute Resolution at the Mine Site

We began by examining the organizational development literature about changing a high-conflict situation into one where conflict is handled in a problem-solving fashion. One approach, called interpersonal peacemaking, uses a third party to help disputants directly confront conflict and resolve it.[16] Because this approach would require a third-party facilitator at each mine site, at least until the parties developed new ways of dealing with one another, we did not think that it was feasible on a large-scale basis. We wanted to recommend changes that the parties could implement themselves.

Another approach, called intergroup training, also relies on a third party to reduce conflict. It restructures perceptions and changes attitudes through workshop training.[17] We were skeptical about this approach because of the vast literature showing that attitudes changed in workshop training do not transfer to the workplace.[18] Additionally, we thought that mine management and union officials needed not just new attitudes but a whole new behavioral repertoire—new procedures, new skills to make them work, and the motivations and resources to use them. It seemed naive to think that even with appropriate attitudes, parties who had been engaging in the fiercest adversarial disputing would know how to engage in problem-solving, interest-based negotiations. We were confident that if we could get miners and mine management to take a problem-solving approach, attitudes would change accordingly.[19] But how to get them to take such an approach?

Management's Tasks. The first step was to get management to deal with disputes at the mine site, rather than sending them to step 3 or arbitration. We thought that the possibility for an interests-based resolution would increase if disputes were dealt with by the parties directly involved. We made two recommendations to accomplish this goal. The first focused on motivation. We advised companies to make a mine manager's strike record an important element of his performance appraisal. We thought that if managers knew that they were being evaluated on their labor relations record, they would be motivated to devote more time and effort to labor relations. Although they might not resolve all disputes, they would be more likely to engage in interests- and rights-based negotiations. We further suggested that foremen be given increased power to resolve grievances; in order to motivate them to use that power, we suggested that their grievance record be an element of their performance appraisal.

Our second recommendation focused on separating the labor relations function from that of mine operations. At the mines we studied, the superintendent was responsible for labor relations as well as operations. We thought that separating these functions would give labor relations more attention. The performance of a person whose job was labor relations would of necessity be evaluated according to the quality of labor relations at the mine. Such a person could also be selected for his interpersonal and negotiating skills, rather than expertise in mine operations.

In retrospect, neither of these suggestions was sufficiently sensitive to management practices in the industry. The first suggestion envisioned changes in performance appraisal systems; in fact, few coal companies had performance appraisal systems to change. In addition, we failed to anticipate the likely resistance by mine managers to being held accountable for strikes that many thought were beyond their control or to giving up control over the labor relations function. Our error was in failing to involve the parties in the process of developing recommendations. Had we done so, they surely would have pointed out the weaknesses of the suggestions and perhaps would have helped us develop better ones. We were not at that time thinking of ourselves as systems designers with a responsibility for implementing our suggested changes. As academics raising issues for practitioners, it never occurred to us to involve the parties in developing the recommendations.

Union's Tasks. Our most radical recommendation was to amend the UMWA constitution to provide that no miner should engage in a strike unless the strike had been authorized in a secret-ballot vote by a majority of the miners employed at the mine, and that any miner who did engage in an unauthorized strike would be subject to discipline, including expulsion from the union. At the time, the UMWA constitution contained neither provision.[20] On the basis of our findings that miners believed few strikes concerned issues worth striking for, and that they struck primarily to support a fellow miner, we thought the number of strikes could be reduced by requiring majority-rule strike authorization. We also thought that if the union adopted and enforced a majority-rule provision, the coal companies might agree not to impose disciplinary sanctions or seek damages for those strikes authorized by majority vote. Both of these ideas were subsequently refined and re-introduced at Caney Creek, where they were central to our efforts to reduce the likelihood of strikes.

Arbitration

We thought that it was important to increase the miners' confidence in arbitration, but we did not have any good ideas about how to do so. Although miners complained about the delay in getting a decision, in fact the procedure was faster than arbitration in other industries. It occurred to us that if we could not increase the miners' confidence in arbitration, we might reduce their dependence on it by reducing the number of grievances taken to arbitration. Union officials, who were elected by the rank and file, were reluctant to deny a miner with a grievance this final opportunity for voice. The political pressure on the union representatives to take weak cases to arbitration might be reduced if they were appointed to office, as they had been before 1972, when Arnold Miller became president. However, the election of district representatives had been one of the major reforms of the Miller administration, and there was no likelihood of a return to the prior system. We did not come up with a satisfactory way to reduce the number of grievances taken to arbitration until the development of grievance mediation several years later.

Conclusion

We distributed our wildcat strike report widely. We sent copies to the presidents of the Bituminous Coal Operators' Association and the UMWA, to all UMWA district presidents, to the labor relations managers at all the companies from which we had requested data, and to the local managers and union officials at the four mines at which we had conducted the field study.

The response was modest. We testified about wildcat strikes before the President's Commission on Coal.[21] But until Caney Creek, no company or local union asked us to come in and work with mine committees or mine managers. There our findings about the causes of wildcat strikes served as a diagnostic model, and many of our recommendations from the wildcat strike study were refined and implemented there. The wildcat strike study, then, served as our initial effort, albeit crude, as systems designers.

It is unlikely that many systems designers will have the opportunity to engage in as broad-based a diagnosis as we did in the wildcat strike study. The parties to a distressed dispute resolution system are unlikely to see the benefits of studying relationships other than their own. They are also unlikely to be willing to wait for the results of such a diagnosis (or to pay for them). Still, the scope of the diagnosis should be related to the scope and severity of the problem. The designer should do what he can to persuade disputants that basing recommendations on hasty and superficial diagnosis is inviting failure.

❖❖❖

Chapter 6

Designing a Low-Cost Dispute System

Intervention at a Strike-Ridden Coal Mine

By March 1980, labor-management strife at Caney Creek mine in eastern Kentucky had reached monumental proportions. In the preceding two years, the miners had engaged in twenty-seven wildcat strikes. Management had responded by firing miners and taking the union to court for breach of contract. In the end, 115 miners had gone to jail for a night. This not only failed to stop the strikes but led to a wave of bomb threats, sabotage, and theft. Miners started bringing guns in their cars when they came to work. Caney Creek was probably the most strife-torn coal mine in the industry at the time.

Senior officials of the company that operated the mine were at a loss. They were seriously considering closing the mine altogether. In March, as a first step and a warning, they laid off a third of the work force. Senior union officials were deeply worried. The layoffs were a serious blow. They were also concerned that, if the miners were jailed again, mines all over the nation might strike in sympathy. Yet they had little influence over the local union. Most senior union and management officials agreed that the conflict was utterly intractable.

101

In this climate, we were invited to consult with union and management about the wildcat strike problem. Our consultation lasted six months. We diagnosed the situation, designed a program of changes with the parties, and participated actively in putting it into place. Our aim was to change the pattern of dispute resolution so that disputes would be handled more satisfactorily and at lower cost to both sides. In short, we served as dispute systems designers.

Getting Started

In late February 1980, Goldberg received a phone call from the president of the union district in which Caney Creek was located and the manager of industrial relations for the coal company that managed Caney Creek. They gave him a brief history of the conflict and expressed their strong concern that the mine might be closed down. They asked Goldberg to come to the mine to consult about the wildcat strike problem. Two weeks later, Goldberg agreed and obtained the parties' consent to include Brett and Ury in the consultation. The company and the union agreed to split the costs.

The parties turned to us, a third party, as a last resort. Union and management were caught in a "hurting stalemate"—neither side could win—and the situation promised only to get worse. Both sides had a clear stake in keeping the mine open. They turned to Goldberg as a neutral outsider because they knew of his arbitration work in the industry and his research with Brett on the causes of wildcat strikes. They wanted him to make recommendations on the basis of his knowledge and neutrality.

As we became involved in the conflict, we realized that the parties' motives for seeking help were complex and varied. Neither the local union officials nor local management—the actual disputants—thought they needed outside help. We were imposed on them by their respective superiors and allies, who felt acutely the costs of the conflict yet felt constrained from intervening more forcefully themselves.

The union district officials had exhorted the miners not to strike, but to little avail. Because they were elected officials, they were reluctant to apply too much pressure. They were hoping that as outsiders we could take the heat for them by telling the miners to make unpopular changes. Top company officials also felt constrained. They were frustrated at their inability to stop the strikes, yet they hesitated to act any more directly than they already had for fear of demoralizing mine management. Moreover, top officials were divided. Sexton, the labor relations manager, advocated replacing certain managers with more diplomatic types; Williams, the operations manager, urged a get-tough policy.[1] Sexton asked our assistance with the unspoken hope that our recommendations would run parallel to his and would help him win the internal debate.

The federal court was also a factor for both parties. The company had filed a suit against the union for striking in violation of the labor agreement. Both company officials and union district officials were anxious to show the court that they were doing something. Each hoped that the third parties would point the finger at someone other than themselves. The parties had many reasons, then, for bringing us in. But, interestingly, no one was very optimistic that our intervention would actually remedy the wildcat strike situation.

The lesson for the dispute systems designer is to probe for why he has been invited into a situation and by which particular players. Changing the way disputes are handled may not be the only or even the main purpose in the parties' minds. The parties may have hidden as well as conflicting agendas. Moreover, some parties who are critical to the ultimate success of the change effort may not have been consulted about the invitation or may have opposed it but been overruled. Typically, it is only as a last resort that parties turn to outsiders. The outsiders, they fear, may meddle. And even if the meddling does reduce the high costs of disputes, it may also threaten one party's interests—which, to the parties, may seem more important than the cost of the disputes.

Diagnosing the Existing Dispute Resolution System

We arrived at our preliminary diagnosis after intensive interviews with virtually all union and management leaders at both the local and higher levels. Subsequently, Ury interviewed more than a hundred miners, studied the files on all written grievances in the mine's history, and observed the mine in its daily and nightly workings for eight weeks.

Understanding the Background of the Disputes

Our diagnosis began by examining the conflict as the union and management saw it. For each side, the problem was the other side's aggressive actions; its own hostile actions were merely a response to provocation. Local management placed the blame primarily on a small group of troublemakers at the mine, including Ratliff, the local union president. Union officials blamed Kilgore, the underground mine superintendent. Moreover, Ratliff and Kilgore had a long-festering personal dispute that they carried on away from work as well as at work.

Whereas the interpersonal conflict was obvious, the issues in contention were not immediately apparent. The conflict resembled an old Kentucky feud where the original issues were largely forgotten; the fighting was fueled instead by motives of reaction and revenge for the actions the other side had taken. Management suspended miners because they struck; the miners struck because management suspended them. Each side set out to teach the other a "lesson." The question became who would let themselves be pushed around—"abused," as the miners put it, "blackmailed," as local management saw it. Each side had become convinced that talk was useless and that the only message the other side understood was force.

Mapping Out the Dispute Resolution Pattern

The mine's dispute resolution pattern was similar to those we found at the high-strike mines in our wildcat strike study. When a miner had a problem, he perceived only two meaningful choices: to lump it or to provoke a walkout. The third option—talking it out—had been seriously undercut. Most miners had lost whatever faith they had had in the grievance procedure, except as a means of harassing management. According to Sexton there was no give and take, no "safety valve," no "shock absorbers." Describing mine management, he said "Everyone says no. They think they're communicating, but they're not. They're dictating, speeching, talking cliches."

The miners were striking less out of irrational rage than out of a perception that they had no other choice. A miner's decision to follow his fellow miners out on strike might sound roughly like this: "If I don't strike, I break my union pledge of solidarity and expose those who do strike to retaliation by management. I risk getting beaten by the other miners or verbally abused or having my property damaged. I stay frustrated and resentful. We let the company abuse us and get away with it."

The data available on grievance procedures revealed a dispute resolution pattern shaped like an inverted pyramid, as shown in Figure 2 in Chapter One. In the sixteen months from March 1978 to July 1979, the miners raised forty-five grievances at step 2.[2] Fourteen grievances were resolved at step 2, sixteen at step 3, fifteen through arbitration, and eighteen through strikes—a topsy-turvy dispute resolution pattern in which the less costly procedures were used the least, and the more costly procedures were used the most.

This pattern appeared in the very first grievance that the union filed after the mine opened. Management had announced an opening for a mobile equipment operator, an above-ground job highly prized by miners at an underground mine. Many miners believed that they could easily do the job, but they could not meet the strict technical qualifications required by management. They thought that management was unfairly keeping the job away from them to give it to a newcomer.[3] The union filed a grievance. Management responded that the contract gave them the right to define job qualifications. The case subsequently went to arbitration.

The arbitrator denied the grievance. Management gloated—they had won their first dispute with the union; the union was not going to tell them how to run *their* mine. The miners felt bitter. In their view, management was fiddling with the job-bidding procedure, assigning jobs without taking into account the miners' legitimate claims. Thus began the puncturing of the miners' initial goodwill toward the company.

This dispute and subsequent ones incurred high costs. The transaction costs included the money and time spent on arbitration, the lost wages for the miners when they struck, the lost output for management, and the jobs lost in the layoff. Both sides also reported dissatisfaction with the outcomes of the disputes. The working relationship between management and union was under heavy strain; indeed, the threatened closure of the mine portended a sharp end to the relationship. And disputes often recurred. Arbitration or strikes rarely brought about a lasting resolution. The underlying problems and resentments were not dealt with, contributing to further grievances and wildcat strikes.

Overall, Caney Creek was a model of a distressed dispute resolution system. Interests-based procedures, such as problem-solving negotiation, were nonexistent. The procedures used focused either on rights, such as arbitration, or on power, such as strikes.

The Critical Motivations

In diagnosing the dispute system still further, we asked why the miners struck so frequently. One central reason, we found, was that management frequently violated the miners' expectations of fairness. This occurred not only in the dispute over the mobile equipment operator's job but in case after case thereafter.

These expectations of fairness, which management ignored, constitute what may be called the "informal contract."[4] The formal written contract represents only part of the normative rules governing the working relations between miner and management. Another part is the nonformalized expectations that miners and managers have. The miner expects fair treatment, a reasonable opportunity for desirable jobs, and flexibility of work rules to take account of individual needs. The manager expects a fair day's work for a fair day's pay.

At Caney Creek, management by and large refused to consider claims based on the informal contract (called "gripes"). Neither the grievance procedure nor any other procedure dealt with such claims. The grievance procedure, moreover, tended to deprive the miner of a sense of control and of a voice in the process. It took control of the grievance out of his hands and gave it to the mine committee, the union district representative, and ultimately the arbitrator (who most miners believed was biased against them). The procedure took a long time, typically months, including many hours of meetings. Perhaps most significantly, the grievance procedure transformed the miner's problem into a contractual grievance that often bore little resemblance to the original problem. The grievant passively watched as others debated his grievance—a debate frequently employing legalistic terms that the miner could not understand.

This point was perhaps best expressed by a mine manager from West Virginia, discussing his own formerly strike-plagued mine:

> We found if we had to go to step 3, a group of strangers appeared on the property—and not real strangers but district representatives from the union [and] labor relations people from my company. . . . [T]hese people . . . more or less took charge of the procedures and things started getting distorted a little bit.
>
> These people . . . have to justify their existence so they feel a need to add a lot of things. We started losing sight of the issues.
>
> The real tragedies came when it became necessary to go to arbitration. Everything gets completely out of context at arbitrations. It is impossible for anyone to win. Arbitrators . . . do

not really find out what the problem was in the
beginning.[5]

In other words, people with other interests entered the picture
and reframed the issue, making it difficult to focus on the
original disputants' underlying interests and to resolve the
dispute to their satisfaction.

Most strikes at Caney Creek concerned the informal
contract, either directly, when miners struck in response to
management's apparent violation of this contract, or indirectly, when they struck in response to management's attempt
to suppress dissatisfaction over such a perceived violation.
When one miner failed to get an outside job, other miners
struck not only out of solidarity but also because they felt
that management had broken the informal contract's promise
of fair treatment, thus threatening their own prospects as well
as those of their aggrieved fellow union member.

The strikes fulfilled significant functions. They gave
the miners a sense of control over the outcome of their grievance and a strong voice in the process. Disgruntled miners
could take action immediately and play a leading role in the
procedure. Although the strikes often failed to win satisfaction of the original claim, they did give the miners a chance
to vent their emotions and to warn management against tres-
passing on their rights in the future.

In sum, then, a miner with a claim saw a choice
between a rights procedure—the grievance procedure—and a
power procedure—the strike. The grievance procedure could
not address the informal contract; a strike could. The grievance procedure deprived the miners of voice and control; the
strike restored them. A third choice, interests-based negotiation, was not available. Little wonder, then, that Caney Creek
was beset by wildcat strikes.

Designing an Effective System

Don't Try to Settle the Conflict, Change the System

The parties' own diagnoses of the problem focused on
people. Thacker, the mine manager, wanted to identify and

fire the troublemakers. The local union wanted to get rid of
Kilgore, the underground mine foreman. Even Sexton, the
company's labor relations manager, had hinted that Kilgore
would have to be transferred or fired. We might have pro-
ceeded from there, deciding whether to recommend firing
individuals. A common response to structural conflict is to
attribute it to personalities and to replace people.[6] The replace-
ments, however, may simply continue the conflict, since the
situation and incentives remain the same. So we groped for
another approach.

The situation seemed ripe for dispute systems design.
Here was a relationship in crisis, indeed on the verge of dis-
solution. The strikes and disciplinary actions—the process of
dealing with the disputes—had become more troublesome
than the substantive issues. We knew we could not resolve the
underlying structural conflict between labor and management, but we thought we could help them find a better way
of handling disputes. Our goals were, first, to identify the
functions served by the power contests—the strikes—and, second, to design a means of fulfilling those functions at lower
cost to the parties. In sum, we sought not to settle the conflict
but to change the system.

We decided not to follow the parties' cue and get rid of
people who were "causing" the conflict. Instead, we focused
on restoring the "talking out" option, which had disappeared
from the repertoire of dispute resolution procedures. The challenge was, to use a term from the wildcat strike study, to build
a "problem-solving relationship" in which disputes would be
resolved primarily by interests-based negotiation. New procedures would not be enough; the changes would require attention to the parties' motivation, skills, and resources.

Prescription: Problem-Solving Negotiation

One of our original ideas was to make the grievance
procedure faster and less expensive. An efficient grievance
procedure, we thought, ought to be able to resolve the grievances that were producing wildcat strikes. Closer inspection,
however, showed us that the problems were more complex.

The grievance procedure did not deal with alleged violations of the informal contract, and it deprived the miners of a sense of control over their grievances. Simply making the procedure more efficient would not alleviate these shortcomings. In short, we realized that motivation is as important as procedure. The designer must carefully analyze why the parties use high-cost dispute resolution procedures. Otherwise, the designer may increase the efficiency of procedures, such as the contractual grievance procedure, that the parties view as poor substitutes for the high-cost procedures.

A better alternative, which took the parties' motivations into account, was suggested by the wildcat strike study: a problem-solving approach to disputes. Grievances at Caney Creek were handled adversarially. The focus remained almost exclusively on contractual rights. The result was a victory for one side and a loss for the other. Problem-solving negotiation, in contrast, emphasizes cooperation, focuses primarily on interests, involves a great deal of mutual persuasion and accommodation, and seeks a mutually satisfactory outcome.

Problem-solving negotiation presented a number of specific advantages. It could deal with disputes stemming from the informal contract, as well as the formal contract. It could focus on the interests that underlay claimed violations of both contracts, and it could do so in workplace terms that were comprehensible to the miners. It could clarify the informal contract, not just for one dispute but for the relationship as a whole. It could take place at a lower level, entail less delay, and allow more active participation by the grievant. In sum, problem-solving negotiation could serve three crucial functions of a wildcat strike: dealing with the informal contract, giving the grievant a sense of control over the outcome, and giving him a voice in the process.

Redesigning the Dispute Resolution Procedures

We began looking for ways to encourage the use of a problem-solving approach. Our discussions with the parties and among ourselves suggested the following changes:

Consultation and Negotiation. Early communication and consultation could help each side understand the interests of the other, and thereby prevent unnecessary disputes. We suggested that top mine management spend as much time as possible underground, listening to the miners' problems. We also thought that management should make it a practice to consult with local union leaders before making any significant changes in working conditions. In addition, we recommended that management and union leaders meet with the miners to discuss general problems and to explain agreed-upon policies. Such interaction, we believed, would create a feeling of participation and partnership, enable management to carry out needed changes with minimal disruption, and prevent many disputes from arising.

We also believed that some disputes could be prevented by the provision of information to the miners. One of the most sensitive issues in the mine was disciplinary suspensions. Management typically pulled aside a miner, told him in private that he was suspended for a specific period, and sent him home. Often rumors spread that the miner had been fired, and a strike resulted. The union officials suggested that such strikes might be averted if a mine committee member, someone the miners trusted, were present at every suspension so that he would have accurate, credible information with which to dispel rumors. So that a committee member could be present, the union officials asked management to notify the mine committee before suspending a miner. We suggested incorporating this change in procedure as an additional means of preventing disputes.

We made several suggestions for dealing with disputes that did arise. The miners needed a way to complain about violations of the informal contract. We suggested that management announce explicitly that they would entertain non-contractual complaints as well as grievances. Motivation also had to be considered. Many miners feared that if they filed a grievance, their foreman would retaliate by giving them undesirable work assignments. The company, we proposed, could help dispel these fears by announcing that it would discipline (and in some cases even discharge) any foreman caught retaliating against a miner for filing a grievance.

Once a dispute emerged, we wanted parties to settle it as close to the point of origin as possible, ideally between a miner and his foreman. We suggested that management encourage foremen to settle grievances by making labor relations a major aspect of the foremens' performance evaluation. We also proposed that the union refuse to take a grievance to step 2 until the miner had raised it with his foreman.

Changing the Procedure for Strikes. To keep disputes from turning into strikes, we proposed adding a prestrike negotiation procedure. In the event of a threatened strike, the miners would continue to work while the mine committee discussed the dispute with management. This provided a cooling-off period and opened the way for negotiation. It is a good example of a "loop-back," a procedure that directs the disputants away from a more costly procedure toward a less costly one.

After the prestrike negotiation, we suggested adding another procedure to filter out some strikes. The union members would discuss the issue and vote on whether to strike. If a majority voted against a strike, the miners would go to work even if a minority still insisted on walking out. This would prevent a minority from leading a strike against the wishes of the majority.

The union leaders pointed out two obstacles to such a procedure. First, they said, if they met to discuss a pending strike, they would be subjected to a possible jail sentence for violating the court's injunction against striking. Avoiding strike discussions was a way to protect themselves. We asked whether they would attend strike meetings if management agreed not to seek penalties against them. They said yes. The second obstacle was that partial walkouts would violate the principle of union solidarity. When one or two miners went home, the other miners automatically followed, not necessarily because they agreed on the issue but because they wanted to protect the strikers. If a few people walked off the job, they might be discharged. If all the miners struck, no one would be discharged. Here again, motivation was a critical factor. Ratliff, the union president, suggested that the majority of the miners would continue to work if management agreed not to discipline those who walked out. When we offered to urge this proposal on management, Ratliff was incredulous: "If you get this for us, the men will kiss your ass at high noon."

If despite these procedures a strike were to occur, we wanted to minimize its costs. This was the goal of our last proposal. Under the existing practice, the first shift out on strike was the first shift to return to work, even if the strike had been settled in time for the intervening shifts to return to work. We recommended that the union abandon this practice in order to reduce the costs to both parties of any strikes that did occur.

In sum, we were trying to change the existing strike procedure in ways that would encourage problem-solving negotiation. We were creating a "loop-back" and trying to create the motivation among union officials and miners to use it. We hoped that these changes would reduce the miners' need to strike by offering a less costly alternative. If the miners were to strike, we tried to reduce the costs of the strike.

Motivating the Parties to Use the New Procedures. In addition to the motivation to use individual procedures, we tried to stimulate motivation to adopt the change program as a whole. Everyone shared an interest in averting further layoffs and in keeping the mine from closing. We suggested that management and union leaders make the severity of the situation clear to the miners. Further strikes would make the mine increasingly unprofitable, leading to additional layoffs and ultimately to the closing of the mine. Conversely, we also recommended that management announce that if the strikes ended the rise in productivity would enable them to rehire miners who had been laid off.

Another element of motivation is the parties' attitudes about each other. We made no recommendations for training that would seek directly to affect these attitudes, because we believed that successful experience with problem-solving negotiation would change attitudes over time. Still, we thought it would be helpful if management encouraged more association between miners and foremen, such as through company sports teams. A common perception at the time was that management was actively discouraging such contact.

Providing the Necessary Skills and Resources. The changes were unlikely to work unless the parties who handled disputes had the skills for problem-solving negotiation. The principal players needed coaching and training. We proposed that Ury remain at the mine for the summer to help people sharpen their communication and negotiation skills. Owing to an interpersonal conflict, however, skill building might not be enough. The two people directly responsible for handling disputes were Kilgore, the underground mine superintendent, and Ratliff, the local union president. In view of their long-standing personal antagonism and their combative personalities, we were skeptical about whether, even with skills training and coaching, they would be able to engage in problem-solving negotiation.

Removing either of these men did not seem feasible. We could not realistically recommend the removal of the union president from office. Nor were we sure that discharging Kilgore, as many people wanted, was a good idea. Although Kilgore had difficulty dealing with people, he seemed to be an excellent production foreman. Moreover, for the company to discharge him could demoralize the other foremen and lead the miners to conclude that they could get rid of any foreman they did not like. Instead of removing either man from his post, we decided to try to ease them both out of the process of handling disputes. We would try to arrange for both Kilgore and Ratliff to withdraw from direct participation in the grievance procedure.

To take over Kilgore's dispute resolution responsibilities, we recommended that management hire a full-time labor relations director whose principal job would be to ensure that the dispute resolution procedures worked well. We suggested that he be available, around the clock if need be, to hear any grievances, whether they stemmed from the formal or the informal contract. His primary approach to any dispute should be problem-solving negotiation. By making him equal in rank to the underground superintendent, the company could both enable him to do his job and signal to the miners that management placed a high priority on good labor relations. Creating a new position at the mine and hiring someone to fill it is an example of providing the resources required for the use of new procedures. To take Ratliff's place in the dispute process, we proposed the elected members of the mine committee. We urged the committee members to encourage miners to raise their grievances instead of lumping them. We recommended that they make themselves available after each shift to listen to any miner's problems and to coach him on how to discuss his problems with management.

In sum, the suggestions we made included procedural changes to encourage interests-based negotiation, as well as measures to enhance the motivation, skills, and resources needed to make the new procedures work.

Negotiating the Changes

Don't Recommend Changes, Negotiate Them

After we had studied the situation, the parties expected us to make recommendations. They wanted to know what was wrong, who was wrong, and what they should do. They expected us to act like arbitrators, except that our judgment would not be binding.

We felt, however, that it was premature to offer definitive recommendations. For one thing, we wanted to take further advantage of the parties' knowledge of their situation. We were also worried that management and union officials might discount our recommendations because of the brevity of our contact with the mine. Moreover, for the proposed changes to be implemented effectively, they needed to be viewed as the parties' own ideas. We concluded that our role included persuading the parties to adopt the ideas. This meant a longer-term intervention, working closely with each side to mediate and implement a program of changes.

We decided to use the one-text mediation procedure described in Chapter Four. After interviewing each side (as we had just done), we would draft a text of suggested actions. Presenting this as a discussion text, not as a recommendation, we would ask the parties for their criticism and advice. We would use their ideas and redraft the text, and then return to them for more criticism and advice. The process would continue until we felt we could no longer improve the text. As the text included more and more of their language and ideas, the parties would, we hoped, think of changes as their own rather than ours.

We decided to work separately with each side at first, developing practices that that side could usefully adopt. We chose this approach not only because of the strained personal relations but also because we did not want the process to become a negotiation with concessions expected from each side, as in collective bargaining. We thought that each side would make changes more easily if the changes were not presented as the other side's demands.

We made three trips to West Virginia and Kentucky to elicit criticism, improvements, and further proposals from union and management.

Trying Out Ideas

We first flew to Charleston, West Virginia, to meet with senior company officials. We began by raising the issue of Kilgore, the underground mine foreman. We stated flatly that we did not recommend discharging or transferring him. Upon hearing this, management officials relaxed and listened with more of an open mind to the suggestions that followed. We then presented a draft text of possible actions for management. Before presenting each suggestion, we first discussed the problem it addressed. We offered suggestions as possibilities to be developed further, not as fixed recommendations. We wanted to elicit their reactions.

On the whole, the meeting went smoothly. Almost everyone reacted favorably to the idea of hiring a full-time labor relations director. The exception was Williams, the operations manager, who declared that the company had played the good guy long enough; he wanted Kilgore to be put in complete charge of labor relations for three months in order to teach the miners some sense. Sexton, the labor relations manager, seemed pleased to have outside support for his conciliatory approach in his ongoing debate with Williams. Thacker, the mine manager, appeared defensive. He said repeatedly that he had already tried to carry out the suggested actions—which, paradoxically, made the suggestions easier to accept.

The next day, we took our one-text to a meeting with union officials at district headquarters. As we had done with management, we presented the possible actions one at a time and asked for criticism. The most controversial suggestions were the new prestrike negotiation and voting procedures. We said that we had not yet raised with management the possibility of an agreement not to discipline miners who engaged in a wildcat strike but that we would do so. In a private conversation with Goldberg, Ratliff agreed to remove himself from an active role in the grievance procedure. With Kilgore and Ratliff both out of the formal procedure, we hoped that it would be easier to initiate problem-solving negotiation.

A Second Round

Within two weeks, management and union both responded favorably to our proposals. The most significant issues remaining to be settled were, for the union, the prestrike procedure and, for management, the guarantees of immunity to union officials and strikers.

Meanwhile, events at the mine continued apace. The miners struck for five days in early May over the discharge of a miner accused of theft. Local union leadership came to the mine at midnight and tried to dissuade the men from striking, but with no success. Management took the local union to federal district court. The judge ordered the union to get the miners back to work within forty-eight hours, or else, he said, he might jail the entire local. The miners returned to work before the deadline. A week later, the judge met with Sam Church, then president of the United Mine Workers, and Harrison Combs, his general counsel, to discuss the deteriorating situation. Union officials told the judge about our efforts. Anxious to keep the matter out of court, the judge offered his enthusiastic support.

Several days after this, we flew to Charleston to meet again with senior company officials. We discussed a number of minor modifications of the suggested actions and then raised the highly sensitive question of the strike procedure. A key issue in the national coal miners' strike of 1977–78 had been whether local unions should have the right to strike during the contract term if a majority of the local voted to do so. The UMWA wanted this right to be included in the labor contract. The mine operators had opposed it and ultimately won. Now, though we did not phrase it that way, we were asking management at Caney Creek to give the local union the right to strike that the UMWA as a whole had been denied.

We presented the proposal as a means of preventing strikes. Strikers would be immune from discipline only if the strike were preceded by a meeting between union leaders and management, as well as a union meeting where the miners would vote. If a majority voted to strike, management would have no authority to discipline the strikers. If a majority voted not to strike, they would work even if a minority struck. The minority who struck after a majority vote to the contrary would not be disciplined as long as they returned to work within twenty-four hours. This, the local union leadership had assured us, would permit the majority to work without fear of subjecting the striking minority to discipline. Furthermore, we had been assured, if the minority saw that the strike failed to attract other miners, they would return to work within twenty-four hours, thus protecting themselves against discipline.

Court sanctions posed an additional obstacle. If union leaders feared court sanctions, they probably would not attend the prestrike meeting. Their presence, we told management, was essential to ensure that the meeting was conducted in a democratic and responsible fashion. So we suggested that the company should also promise not to use leaders' participation in a strike meeting as a basis for seeking court sanctions against them. In explaining our recommendations, we said: "What do you have to lose? The miners have been striking anyway. You don't want them to go to jail again. If this measure has a chance of preventing strikes, why not?" Management officials eventually agreed to provide the necessary guarantees on an experimental basis.

In these negotiations, we were not only mediators but also designers and advocates of a particular procedure. This required a balancing act among disparate roles.

Reaching Agreement

Upon our return to Boston, we redrafted the proposals yet again. We tried to cast most of the changes as independent and unilateral actions by one side rather than as agreements, in order to emphasize that these were steps worth taking on their own, not concessions exchanged with the other side. We also wanted to keep the program from unraveling if one side failed to live up to one of its new policies. We presented the proposals in four documents: an internal memorandum from the company president to Caney Creek management detailing the new labor relations policies and practices; a statement of the new policies from management to the miners; an agreement between management and the local union on the strike procedure; and a statement of policy from the union to management.

In the middle of June, we took the documents to Caney Creek. We first went over the draft union statement and the draft union-management agreement with union officials, who agreed, with considerable enthusiasm, to adopt both. The next morning, we met with mine management and top company officials to discuss management's draft statement and the draft strike procedure. Few problems arose, as the issues had been well worked out in advance. That afternoon, two dozen union and management officials met at Caney Creek. Thacker read aloud management's statement, and Ratliff read the union statement. Then each read their half of the agreement. Everyone seemed in good spirits. Both Ratliff and Sexton predicted that if this agreement worked at Caney Creek, the strike procedure would be adopted into the next national contract. The union district leadership expressed strong support for the agreement and privately expressed surprise that management had been so generous.

Ratliff and the district president signed the agreement for the union, and the company president and Thacker signed for management. Photographs were taken. The atmosphere was like that at the signing of a peace treaty. The participants said they felt that were making coal industry history.

Putting the Changes into Place

The Ratification Vote

Management and union still needed to introduce the new procedures to the foremen and the miners. The day after the signing ceremony, Thacker presented and explained the procedures to the foremen. He also introduced Ury and explained that he would spend the summer at the mine helping to implement the changes.

We wanted the miners to learn about the new procedures and acquire a sense of ownership over them, so we suggested submitting the agreement to them for formal ratification. Union and management agreed. The day after the signing ceremony, the statements and the agreement were mailed to all the miners. The next day, Ratliff introduced Ury to the miners, explaining that he was there to learn about the situation and to help them in any way he could.

Later that day, a large measure of our optimism evaporated. Ratliff confided to Ury that he did not think the agreement would pass. Most miners, he said, did not trust management to keep its pledges not to retaliate against a grievant and not to discipline strikers. They felt that they had been tricked before, and they were determined not to fall into a trap again. Moreover, because there had not been a strike in five weeks, what need existed for the agreement?

Ratliff's own support for the agreement began to crumble when he read the signs of opposition. He began to voice doubts himself. When Ury approached him about trying to meet the miners' basic concerns, perhaps even postponing the ratification vote to do so, Ratliff refused. He wanted to have the vote, get it over with, and move on to something else. It seemed as if he thought he had backed a loser and wanted to cut his losses.

Weeks later, Ury learned one reason for the sudden reversal. The local union officials had shown the agreement to their lawyer, whose existence they had never mentioned to us. The lawyer had voiced three objections: (1) making a local agreement set an undesirable precedent; (2) the company could, despite its written pledge, seek court sanctions against union leaders for prestrike meetings; and (3) the company's promise not to discipline strikers might not stand up in court. Moreover, he misinterpreted the company's promise as requiring it only to wait for twenty-four hours before disciplining a miner. In fact, the clause meant that no one could be disciplined for striking—even after a majority vote not to strike—as long as he returned to work within twenty-four hours.

In the third week of June, the miners voted to reject the agreement, 144 to 23. It was a vote of no confidence in management, in the union leadership, and perhaps in us as well.

Why did the miners overwhelmingly reject the carefully negotiated strike agreement? In hindsight, it seems clear that four factors contributed.

First, the rank-and-file miners continued to distrust management. They simply did not believe that management would carry through on its promises. The distrust had not, so far, been diminished by our intervention. A change in attitudes, we realized, may be needed if people are to adopt new procedures. Perhaps we should have had the miners try out the new procedures and see for themselves that management lived up to its commitments before we sought ratification.

Second, unlike the union leadership, the rank-and-file miners had not been involved in developing the agreement. The leadership had failed to consult with them during the process. Although the new procedures would give them more voice and control in dealing with disputes, the rank and file lacked voice and control in the process of reaching agreement itself. Ironically, the agreement foundered on the very problem it was intended to handle.

Third, the agreement was perceived as an addition to the national contract. In coal-mining culture, the contract was venerated almost like the Bible. To add to it was to tamper with it. A number of miners simply announced, "The contract's good enough for me!"

Finally, the local union lawyer's disapproval of the agreement weakened the union leaders' enthusiasm and may have dissuaded them from seeking to overcome the miners' skepticism. The lawyer may have felt peeved at being excluded from the process of redesigning the dispute system. Moreover, the changes in procedure meant a far smaller role for him.

The ratification vote brought home to us the importance of identifying possible opponents to change and finding ways to involve them in the process or, failing that, ways to neutralize their resistance. This task is central to the job of dispute systems design. The ratification vote put the change program in doubt and called for a reassessment of our strategy.

Reassessment and Redesign

The day after the vote, Ury went to Ratliff's house and spoke with him about his evident abandonment of the agreement. Ratliff explained that the miners had rejected the agreement because they regarded any agreement with management other than the national contract as unwise. But, he added, the agreement could still be implemented informally. When a strike threatened, for instance, he would meet with management and organize a discussion among the miners. Moreover, he and other union leaders would work even if a strike did take place.

Management also accepted the idea of informal implementation. Sexton, the company's labor relations manager, said that the company would adhere to its commitments. So, after the shock of the miners' rejection of the agreement, it looked as if the program of changes would continue as planned. The one exception was that the prestrike procedure would be not a written agreement but rather a modus vivendi to which both sides would seek to adhere.

Establishing Ury's Role

Given the level of suspicion at the mine, neither local management nor the union trusted Ury at the outset. His biggest credibility problem was with the rank-and-file miners, because his background and social class placed him closer to management than to the union. To begin to overcome the miners' distrust and to learn as much as he could about the mine, Ury asked to be taken underground. He was outfitted in miner's garb and given safety instructions. Miners wore black hard hats, and management wore white hard hats; Ury requested a green hard hat to signal his neutrality. He spent three consecutive days in the coal mine, on the day and evening shifts, trying to meet all the miners.

Ury also moved his belongings from the management locker room to the miners' bathhouse. His purpose was twofold: to identify himself with the miners and to have an excuse to be where most of the interaction among miners took place. His entry was not without incident. Upon seeing him, one miner exclaimed openly, "What's he doing in here? Let's string him up!"

On the whole, though, miners and foremen responded favorably to Ury's coming down into the mine. Pleasantly surprised that he showed an interest in their work, they taught him to operate the mining machines and told him about their jobs. A few miners insisted on putting him through the coal miners' initiation of "hairing," a ritual in which a group of miners forcefully cut a few pubic hairs from the struggling initiate. Word that he'd been "haired" spread rapidly among the other miners, producing a change in attitude and such comments as, "Now you're an official coal miner. You're a regular guy!"

Ury also spent time with foremen and managers, questioning them about their jobs and the operations of the mine. He wanted not only to learn what he could but also to demonstrate that he was interested in management's concerns as well as those of the miners.

Ury began to build personal relationships with Ratliff and Thacker. He lunched with Ratliff, played pool with him, met his wife and children, practiced shooting with him, and went on an all-night fishing trip with him and other union leaders. He also dined with Thacker and his family and attended his son's birthday party. He wanted to win each leader's confidence and gain the personal rapport that would allow him to give them frank feedback without their taking offense.

Implementing the Procedures Informally

Despite the miners' rejection of the strike agreement, union and management began to implement most of the changes to which they had committed themselves. Management hired a full-time labor relations director with authority to settle grievances and made certain that a mine committee member was present whenever a suspension was discussed. The union made a mine committee member available on each shift to discuss grievances. Moreover, management began to consult with union leaders before taking controversial actions and even started to consult with rank-and-file miners about certain troublesome problems.

The change is best illustrated by the company's adoption of a bomb-threat policy. The second week that Ury was there, an anonymous caller announced that he had placed a bomb in the mine and set it to go off at the change of shifts. Management told the incoming miners about the threat. Thirty-seven of forty-four chose not to work, losing a shift's pay as a result. Ury suggested to Thacker that he ask the miners for their advice, because they too had an interest in deterring bomb threats that prevented them from working. Thacker did so when a second bomb threat took place a few days later. One miner suggested playing the tape recording that management had made of the threat. Thacker agreed, hoping that even if the miners would not identify the caller to management, they might deal with him themselves. This time, in contrast to all previous bomb threats, almost all the miners worked after the mine was searched.

Once the miners were involved in trying to solve the problem, bomb threats started to lose credibility with them. They began to see the threats as someone's attempt to stop them from working and earning their pay. In several subsequent threats that summer, the great majority of the miners worked straight through.

Other planned changes were also carried out. As agreed, Ratliff and Kilgore gave up their roles in the grievance procedure. Both management and union leaders encouraged the miners to express their problems, and the miners reported no retaliation for doing so. Management carried out its promise to rehire laid-off miners as the strikes ceased and productivity increased. Kilgore organized a picnic for union and management, which signaled management's commitment to greater social association between miners and managers.

The prestrike procedures were carried out in the one situation that threatened to turn into a strike that summer. Instead of walking out, the miners remained in the bathhouse until Ratliff had discussed the issue with Thacker. Ratliff came back with management's proposed solution, and the miners decided not to strike.

In short, as agreed upon, management and union increased the opportunities for interests-based negotiation and implemented changes designed to bring grievances to the surface and resolve them.

The Designer as Coach

That summer at the mine, Ury focused on the process of handling disputes, not the merits of individual disputes.

He did not act as a mediator in the ordinary sense of the term. He did not run meetings and rarely made substantive suggestions. Rather, he helped to implement the new procedures. He spent each day at the mine talking with management, union leaders, and the rank and file. He listened for and identified emerging complaints and disputes. He ensured that meetings took place promptly and that problems were thoroughly aired. He attended almost every meeting about a dispute, and he strongly urged each side to give problem-solving negotiation a chance.

Ury's restrained role is illustrated by one of the first issues to arise. Moses Kinder, a miner recently recalled from layoff, complained that someone junior to him on the seniority ladder had been recalled three weeks before he had. Kinder sought back pay for the three weeks for which he claimed he had been improperly denied work. When he raised the issue with his mine committee member, the committee member told him to talk to his foreman first, just as the union leaders had promised they would do.

When Ury learned of the grievance, he brought it up with Lucas, the new labor relations director for Caney Creek. A former union official from Harlan County, Lucas had arrived only a few days earlier. Lucas met with Kinder. Ury was present, but he limited his role to clarifying each side's point of view to the other and ensuring that the problem was handled promptly. Lucas decided that the company had made a mistake and agreed to pay Kinder the $2,000 owed to him. Previously, management would probably have fought such a grievance all the way to arbitration. In settling the case, Lucas created a favorable impression among the miners; they perceived him as fair and as having the authority to settle grievances.

On a few occasions, Ury felt it necessary to become actively involved, because the parties had a long-standing habit of treating the negotiation steps either as pro forma or as an opportunity to assert their own rights and castigate the other side. This was particularly true at the first formal grievance meeting held during his stay at the mine. Ury thought it especially important that this grievance be settled to everyone's satisfaction, in order to convince people that problem-solving negotiation could work.

The grievance was brought by James Robinette, a night-shift electrician assigned to the above-ground maintenance shop. He complained that he had been assigned to fix machines underground every night for the previous two weeks. He wanted management to allocate some of the repair work to the night shift, so that he could work above ground part of the time. Although there was little basis in the formal contract for his claim, Robinette thought it was unfair—a violation of the informal contract—to make an above-ground electrician work underground when there was work that he could do in the shop. Management was reluctant to grant the request. A maintenance foreman represented management at step 2 of the grievance procedure. He said that an unusual number of maintenance problems had arisen and that the night shift had a high absenteeism rate. Accordingly, he explained, management needed maintenance people like Robinette more urgently underground "putting out fires" than above ground rebuilding machines.

Ury listened, clarified the problem, and asked occasional questions. When he spotted a possible settlement, he brought it to the parties' attention. At little cost to management, Ury suggested, Robinette's foreman could give him a list of work to do in the shop when he was not needed underground, so that he would not be sent underground just because no shop work had been assigned. This settlement would address Robinette's interest in a fair share of above-ground work, as well as management's interest in having him available for necessary underground work. Robinette said that the proposal satisfied him. The maintenance foreman was resistant at first, but he finally agreed. Both sides emerged educated and pleased. Previously, the case would probably have dragged on and produced continuing resentment and possibly a strike. Extremely surprised at the outcome, a mine committee member declared that it was the first grievance in his experience that management had settled at step 2.

As the examples illustrate, Ury's presence had several effects. The mere presence of a third party makes disputants behave more reasonably and creates pressure on them to reach agreement. Ury's presence also underscored the importance of talking out problems and represented each side's commitment to work out differences with the other. He also served as a symbol and reminder of the new procedures. His frequent conversations about the way people were dealing with particular disputes helped teach them the value of problem-solving negotiation. Whenever the parties were focusing on who was right or who was more powerful, Ury tried to shift the focus back to the underlying interests.

In addition to coaching, Ury offered a workshop in problem-solving negotiation for a group of fifteen union officials and managers. The joint training began with a discussion of union and management views of their conflict. Then Ury engaged the participants in a trust exercise which played out the classic "prisoner's dilemma." The group formed two teams, each containing both union and management members. If both teams cooperated, both won; if neither cooperated, both lost. If one cooperated and the other did not, the noncooperator won and the cooperator lost by a big margin. As might be expected, one team told the other that it would cooperate and then double-crossed it. (Interestingly, union president Ratliff engineered the double-crossing strategy.) The group, now realizing how easy it is to develop a high level of distrust, discussed practical means of breaking down distrust at the mine.

Ury followed with a presentation to the group on problem-solving negotiation. He then conducted negotiation exercises in which the participants simulated dealing with difficult grievances and strikes. Union people played management roles and vice versa. Afterward, many participants said that the exercises had helped them realize how difficult the other side's role could be.

Ury not only coached and trained the parties but also served as a watchdog as the new procedures were implemented. His presence prodded the local union and management to try to settle their disputes through problem-solving negotiation. In all these ways, Ury tried to strengthen the new dispute system while it was in its most fragile form. He refrained from becoming actively involved in the mediation of disputes, for fear of making the parties dependent on him. Just as a building needs to stand on its own after the temporary supports are withdrawn, so the new procedures would need to persist after he had departed.

Changes in the Mine's Dispute System

During the summer of 1980, people at the mine resolved their disputes far differently from the way they had in the two previous years. No strikes took place, though there were two strike threats. Nor was there a compensating increase in the number of formal grievances. The union raised only three formal grievances, all concerning job bids, and these were settled at step 2; none went to step 3 or on to arbitration. Instead of debating in an adversarial fashion about contractual rights, the parties began to discuss each other's perceptions, to listen, to focus on underlying interests, and to reason with each other. Interests-based negotiation became a common practice.

Significantly, the change did not result from a policy of appeasement on the part of management. Thacker, for instance, held his ground on one job-assignment issue and persuaded local union officials that they did not have a case. On another occasion, he suspended a miner for absenteeism and convinced the miner, and the mine committee member present, that the punishment was just.

The miners were now willing to give management and their union leadership the benefit of the doubt in potential strike situations. After one threatened strike, union president Ratliff confided to Ury, "I'll tell you one thing that has enthused me about this thing [the program of changes]. Yesterday morning [during the threatened strike], all the men listened to me. They paid attention to what I had to say, and they said, 'Well, let's give them a chance.'"

Taking Leave

By the first week of August, miners were approaching Ury frequently with complaints. He would listen carefully, tell them he would check into it, and guide them to the appropriate union or management official. Instead of acting directly, he was trying to carve out a channel for complaints after he left. He wanted to start reducing dependency on him.

The third week of August was the end of Ury's assignment. He met with the mine communication committee to discuss his analysis and recommendations. He also made a speech to each of the three shifts, stressing that the blame for the mine's troubles lay not on any troublemakers but on poor communication and too little problem-solving negotiation. He congratulated the miners and foremen for the improvement in labor relations and expressed the strong belief that neither the miners nor management were trying to take advantage of the other.

Ury's stay ended with the first Caney Creek picnic, sponsored jointly by the union and the company. Amid feasting and sports, one of the mine foremen and his band played bluegrass and country music. Almost all the principal players in management and the union attended.

Evaluating the Results

Did the New Procedures Work?

Disputes continued to arise at Caney Creek, as well they should given the underlying structural conflict between management and labor. But the dispute resolution pattern changed significantly and remained changed over the eight years since our design effort.

In the year following the redesign of the dispute system, both union and management reported substantial progress. The level of interests-based negotiation remained high: the miners reported that they raised their problems more frequently and that management made greater efforts to deal with them. The level of satisfaction with outcomes increased. Both sides reported a considerable improvement in their working relationship. The mine went more than eleven months without a strike, and the threat of mine closure faded.

There were two near-strikes: one in September 1980, the other in January 1981. In each case, the miners stayed in the bathhouse and refused to go to work. The union leaders met with management to discuss the problem. When the problem was resolved, the miners went to work. They were, in effect, carrying out the prestrike negotiation procedure specified in the original agreement. This, too, was a form of progress.

After almost a year without strikes, they began again. Two occurred in March 1981, both directly connected with national contract negotiations then being conducted. Six more occurred from July 1981 through May 1982. The issues involved included a layoff, a coveted job that was eliminated, and a foreman who got off lightly for hitting a miner. Unlike so many of the issues that had previously led to strikes, these were considered significant by both union and management, who perceived even this as progress over the previous situation.

Occasional strikes continued during the period of the 1984 contract. In the three years and four months during which the contract was in force, the mine experienced five strikes, an average of one every eight months. While not ideal, this was about normal in the coal industry at the time. The issues behind the strikes continued to be perceived as significant. There were no strike threats or bomb threats. The company continued to refrain from going to court. As Lucas, the mine's labor relations director, put it, "Nothing is really settled in court. You still have to go back to the mine to work it out."[7]

Management followed a practice of consultation and of listening to every complaint, whether or not it was based on the formal contract. "When we're talking about grievances, we look at the human side, regardless of whether we're contractually obliged to do so," reported Lucas.[8] He cited the company's practice of posting notices of temporary job openings, which it is not required to do, as well as its practice of training underground miners in above-ground jobs so that, when an opening comes, they can apply for it. The grievance record for the latter half of 1987 was particularly impressive: only three written grievances, all of which were settled at step 2.

It is clear that the effort at dispute systems design led to a major change in the pattern of dispute resolution at Caney Creek. Dispute resolution consumed less money and time; the working relationship improved; and the settlements reached were more satisfactory to each party. In the years since, there have been ups and downs in the relationship, but dispute resolution has remained less costly than it had been previously. As the district representative for the union reflected to us in early 1988, "It changed 98 percent just after you were in there. Up to that point, the least little thing caused a strike. Now they don't strike any more than any other mine. When they do, it's just for a day, not for a week like it used to be. You really made a difference."[9]

Why Did the New Procedures Work?

How can the success at Caney Creek be explained? Two factors are particularly important. First, conditions were ripe for change. The mine had suffered a destructive trauma, and worse was threatened—the closure of the mine. This provided the motivation to try new procedures. Moreover, as several union and management officials had pointed out to us, it was not uncommon for many start-up mines to go through a period of what they called "settling down"; in our terms, they experienced a high number of rights and power contests until the rights and the power balance had become sufficiently clear. After that, fewer disputes arose, and those that did were more easily resolved. Although the situation at Caney Creek had gone on longer and with greater turmoil than anyone could remember happening before, some union and management officials speculated that it was, at the time of our intervention, reaching the point of "settling down."

The second major factor influencing the turnaround was our effort at dispute systems design. We redesigned the dispute procedures, placing special emphasis on increasing the motivation, skills, and resources for interests-based negotiation. Where a rights-based grievance procedure could not meet the functions served by wildcat strikes—dealing with the informal contract, providing a sense of control over the outcome, and allowing for voice—interests-based negotiation could do so. And it could do so at far lower costs than strikes. We also tried to provide a prestrike procedure that would encourage negotiation before striking and, if that failed, at least would shorten the strikes. In sum, we tried to shift the dominant focus from power and rights to interests.

In addition to our design, the process—how we dealt with the parties—was critical. From the very beginning, we involved the principal players in our diagnosis and design, not only to tap their valuable ideas and knowledge but also to organize support for change and to defuse opposition. Our follow-up work in implementation was also essential. We persuaded the disputants to try the new procedures and helped them learn the problem-solving negotiation skills that they needed in order to use the procedures effectively.

At the same time we were working at Caney Creek, Goldberg was designing a grievance mediation procedure that he hoped to institute widely in the coal industry. In good part because of our experience at Caney Creek, Goldberg believed that interests-based mediation might be less costly than rights-based arbitration and better able to uncover and resolve the real problems underlying grievances. Here was a chance to change the dispute resolution system not just of a single mine but of an industry. The following chapter describes this effort.

❖❖

Chapter 7

Cutting Dispute Costs for an Industry

The Grievance Mediation Program

By late 1979, Goldberg, who had been arbitrating in the coal industry for more than five years, had become increasingly frustrated with both the volume and the type of cases he was being called on to decide. Many of them presented issues on which the contract was clear and the decision was obvious. Why, he wondered, were such cases so frequently arbitrated? Another group of cases he wondered about were those in which the costs of arbitration to the company and the union exceeded the amount at stake, and no significant issue of contract interpretation was involved. For example, many grievances went to arbitration in which a miner complained that someone else had been asked to perform Saturday work that should have been assigned to him. If the miner prevailed, he would win approximately $150. The costs of arbitration to both company and union were at least three times that amount. No meaningful precedent was likely to be set, because the standard for the distribution of Saturday work had been in the contract since 1971,[1] and it had been the subject of hundreds of arbitral opinions. Nonetheless, Goldberg was constantly presented with such cases.

134

Goldberg's experience was not unique. In the mid 1970s, arbitration was used far more often in the coal industry than in any other. More than 8,000 cases went to arbitration between 1974 and 1977.[2] Arbitrators' fees alone were in excess of $2,000,000 for this period. Additional costs arose from the lost production time of those involved in arbitration proceedings, as well as various incidental costs—travel, hearing transcripts, document reproduction, and so on. In all, the transaction costs of arbitration in the coal industry were undoubtedly in excess of $1,000,000 per year.

High transaction costs were only a part of the problem. Recurrence was common; essentially the same case would be arbitrated over again. The overburdened system was often slow. As with any adjudicative system, outcomes were win-lose in nature, with little opportunity for joint gain. A substantial majority of the cases were lost by the union, adding to the miners' dissatisfaction with arbitration. Enough cases were lost by employers that they, too, occasionally complained of arbitral incompetence. Finally, frequent arbitration had damaged the union-management relationship. The desire to prevail in arbitration sometimes led one side to make statements or charges to the arbitrator that the other side regarded as unfair. Sometimes this led to retaliatory statements or charges. Even if it did not, the adversarial battling reduced the parties' capacity to work together constructively.

Diagnosing the Existing Dispute Resolution System

The union's heavy reliance on arbitration, Goldberg found, could not be explained in terms of its superior skills or resources. Union representatives were generally less skilled than their company counterparts, who typically had more formal education and training. The union's financial resources to support costly arbitration battles were no greater than those of the major coal companies, with whom most of the arbitrations took place.

Although procedures short of arbitration were available—the first three steps of the contractual grievance procedure—few grievances were resolved at those levels.[3] At steps 1 and 2, the wildcat strike study had shown, many mine managements made no substantial effort to resolve grievances, particularly those based on the informal contract. If, in management's opinion, the miner's claim was not based on contractual right, it was sent on to step 3. If the miner was not satisfied with the results at step 3, the union had powerful incentives to take the grievance to arbitration. For one thing, UMWA field representatives are elected by the members of the locals that they serve, so a grievant could threaten political retaliation against a representative who declined to arbitrate a grievance regardless of its merits. In addition, the UMWA, in common with other unions, owes members a legal duty of fair representation, which it breaches if it fails to arbitrate a grievance for reasons that are arbitrary, discriminatory, or in bad faith.[4] High UMWA officials had told Goldberg that union policy was to arbitrate weak cases whenever a failure to do so might lead to a duty of fair representation claim, and this, too, provided an explanation for both the high volume of arbitration and the appearance at arbitration of cases of little merit.

Company labor relations managers might be similarly motivated to arbitrate weak cases. The labor relations representative frequently reports to an operations manager. If the operations manager believes that the company is contractually in the right, he may insist that the case be arbitrated even when the labor relations representative believes that the company's position will not be sustained at arbitration.

The task of the systems designer in these circumstances (though Goldberg did not think in those terms at the time) was twofold: to encourage the parties to focus on the interests underlying both the grievance and management's response, thus increasing the likelihood of a negotiated resolution; and, for those grievances not settled through negotiation, to provide a procedure that would be less costly than arbitration.

Designing an Effective System

The Initial Concept

Goldberg's initial idea for accomplishing these goals was an advisory arbitration procedure with a mediation component. He had been fascinated by an experiment conducted with labor law students by Robben Fleming, an experienced arbitrator and law teacher. Fleming gave each student the evidence and arguments from a case in which he had been the arbitrator. He then asked each student to study the materials and write a decision. The student's decision matched Fleming's in twelve out of thirteen contract interpretation cases and fifteen out of twenty-three discipline and discharge cases.[5] Fleming concluded that employers and unions should give greater consideration to using inexperienced arbitrators, since their decisions were likely to be the same as those of their more experienced peers.

Fleming's results suggested a different idea to Goldberg. If the decisions of novice arbitrators often matched those of experienced arbitrators, then surely an experienced arbitrator who examined the evidence and heard the arguments should be able to predict how another experienced arbitrator would decide the same case. Goldberg thought that this was particularly likely in the coal industry, where he had found that so many cases presented relatively simple issues. Indeed, he thought that under these circumstances, an experienced arbitrator could accurately predict the outcome after only briefly considering the relevant evidence and arguments. This led to the initial concept of what was ultimately to be grievance mediation. In order to reduce the frequency with which the parties resorted to costly arbitration, a step would be added to the grievance procedure. At this step, which would come after step 3 and before arbitration, an experienced arbitrator would hear a brief presentation of evidence and arguments and then advise the parties of the likely outcome if the case went to arbitration. This nonbinding advisory opinion would be given orally and immediately.

The savings would be substantial. The procedure was so simple that the arbitrator should be able to give three advisory opinions per day. At the then current rate for the most respected arbitrators in the coal industry—approximately $400 per day plus travel expenses—the procedure would be able to dispose of cases for approximately $200, rather than the approximately $1,000 per case being spent for conventional arbitration in the coal industry at the time.

Not only would this procedure be quicker and less expensive than arbitration; it would also reduce the parties' incentives to go to arbitration with cases of little or no merit. If an experienced arbitrator predicted that the company would lose at arbitration, that should enable the company labor relations representative, at least if he agreed with the advisory opinion, should be able to persuade operating personnel to settle the case. Similarly, if the arbitrator were to advise the grievant and the local union that they would lose at arbitration, the force of that opinion, if it was consistent with the opinion of the district representative, should substantially reduce their motivation to arbitrate. The grievant would have had his day in court, and only the most intrepid would insist on a second day in court before a second arbitrator. If the grievant did insist on arbitrating, the union should be able to refuse with little fear of breaching its duty of fair representation. In light of the arbitrator's advisory opinion that it would lose at arbitration, the union's refusal to arbitrate could not be said to be arbitrary, discriminatory, or in bad faith.

Goldberg thought that the advisory opinion approach held great promise as a means of reducing the motivation of step 3 representatives to arbitrate for political or legal reasons. Still, he was aware that it did not deal satisfactorily with cases in which the real issue was not the interpretation of the formal contract but reconciling the conflicting interests that underlay the grievance. Hence, Goldberg envisaged that the third-party neutral would, in addition to providing an advisory opinion, act as a mediator. He would try to help the parties use interests-based negotiation to resolve any underlying claims or problems.

The idea of mediation came primarily from Goldberg's own experience. As an arbitrator, he had from time to time attempted to settle grievances through mediation rather than decide them himself. Those efforts had rarely been successful, but Goldberg thought that the new procedure would work better. For one thing, the participants in Goldberg's arbitration sessions had expected arbitration, not mediation, and so they were not prepared to negotiate a settlement. Participants in the new procedure would arrive with different expectations. Additionally, Goldberg's participants might have been unwilling to disclose their underlying interests to a third party who would be the arbitrator if settlement efforts failed. If the third party had no decisional power but could only give advice, participants might be more forthcoming.

Goldberg believed that the mediation efforts should precede the advisory opinion, and that the advisory opinion should be issued only if settlement negotiations were unsuccessful. Still, he did not have much faith that the mediation procedure would generate settlements without the use of the advisory opinion.

*The Concept Evolves: Mediation as an Aid
to Interests Negotiation*

A number of factors then led Goldberg to place more emphasis on the mediation component of the procedure. Initially, he discussed the new procedure with many colleagues in the winter and spring of 1980. In addition to Brett and Ury, two others were particularly influential: James Healy, a professor at Harvard Business School with many years' experience as an arbitrator and mediator, and William Hobgood, then assistant secretary for labor-management relations in the U.S. Labor Department and previously a mediator with the Federal Mediation and Conciliation Service. Both Healy and Hobgood argued knowledgeably and persuasively that mediation could resolve seemingly intractable disputes, and they urged Goldberg to give greater prominence to mediation in the procedure. In particular, Hobgood argued for using people with substantial mediation experience as the third-party neutrals, so that they would be effective in bringing about settlements through mediation. Another colleague, Harvard Law School professor Paul Weiler, a former chair of the British Columbia Labor Board, described that agency's success in mediating grievances—settling an average of 71 percent of the approximately 600 grievances presented to it annually. Similarly, Goldberg found that some U.S. state mediation agencies reported settlement rates of between 75 and 88 percent.[6]

The most important factor leading to an increased emphasis on mediation was our experience at Caney Creek. There, we saw that many miners preferred the wildcat strike to arbitration because arbitration deprived them of voice and because it failed to deal with the interests that underlay grievances. The miners would probably be equally dissatisfied with a new step in the grievance procedure that gave them no greater voice than did arbitration and that consisted primarily of advisory arbitration concerning the contract. On the other hand, they would probably be more satisfied if the new procedure provided them with substantial voice and emphasized the interests underlying the grievance. Indeed, if it did so, it might even serve as a substitute for the wildcat strike. This, too, argued for an increased emphasis on mediation.

All this led to a substantial change in the proposed procedure. By the late spring of 1980, Goldberg began to see it primarily as mediation, in which the third-party neutral would help the parties reach a mutually acceptable resolution, primarily through interests negotiation. The advisory opinion was retained as a low-cost rights-based component for two reasons. First, when grievances involved a genuine dispute about contract interpretation, he thought that the opinion of an experienced arbitrator would contribute substantially to resolution. Second, since the coal industry had no experience with mediating grievances, he thought that the new procedure would have a better chance of being adopted if it contained a familiar element—a decision, albeit advisory, at the end of the procedure.

*The Concept Refined: Grievance Mediation
as It Was Presented to the Coal Industry*

The procedure proposed to the coal industry in June 1980 was as follows: after step 3 of the grievance procedure, the parties would have the option of taking unresolved grievances to mediation rather than directly to arbitration. The mediation procedure would be informal. The relevant facts would be brought out in a narrative fashion, rather than through examination and cross-examination of witnesses. Legal rules concerning the admission of evidence would not apply. No record of the proceedings would be made. The discussion would not be limited to matters relevant under the terms of the written contract; the parties would be free to raise any fact or argument they thought relevant.

The mediator would be an experienced and respected arbitrator who possessed mediation skills and, if feasible, mediation experience. His primary effort would be to help the parties settle the grievance in a mutually satisfactory fashion. In doing so, he would encourage the parties to consider not only the written contract but also their respective interests. If no settlement appeared possible, the mediator would give an oral opinion concerning the likely outcome at arbitration and explain his reasoning. If the parties still could not resolve the grievance, they would be free to arbitrate. The mediator could not serve as arbitrator, and nothing said or done during mediation, by the parties or the mediator, could be used at arbitration.

We had high expectations for the success of the procedure. We hoped that the mediator would engage the parties in interests-based negotiation and that these negotiations would typically result in agreements satisfactory to both sides. We expected recurrence of disputes to decrease and transaction costs to drop. We also hoped that experience with interests-based mediation would teach the parties how to use an interests-based approach in their day-to-day interactions and that, as a result, they would settle a higher proportion of disputes through direct negotiations, without strikes, arbitration, or even mediation. Indeed, it was even possible that a collaborative approach to dispute resolution might make the parties' overall relationship less adversarial and more cooperative.[7]

For all its theoretical advantages, mediation entailed some risks. The central risk was that it would not resolve grievances. If most mediated grievances went on to arbitration, mediation would simply add to the cost and delay of grievance resolution. We could have avoided that risk by providing that, if mediation did not settle the grievance, the mediator would serve as arbitrator and issue a final, binding decision (the procedure known as "med-arb"). But that approach entailed risks of its own. If the mediator had the power to resolve the dispute, we feared that each party would treat the procedure as primarily rights-oriented and would concentrate on persuading the mediator that it was right, rather than on developing a settlement that met the interests of both. That would eliminate both the short-range advantage of mediation, reaching mutually acceptable outcomes, and its long-range advantage, training the participants in problem-solving skills. Our provision for an advisory opinion created some risk of this; we decided not to increase that risk by permitting the mediator to issue a final and binding decision.[8]

Another risk was that the availability of inexpensive mediation would discourage negotiated settlements earlier in the process. For example, suppose that during the step 3 negotiations, a grievant was offered $200 in settlement of his $500 claim. In the absence of mediation, he might well accept that offer because the only alternative, arbitration, would cost the union approximately $500 and might result in the grievance being denied altogether. If mediation were available, at a cost to the union of only $150, the grievant might reject the offer of $200, calculating that the additional costs were not great, that he could do no worse at mediation, and that he might do better. If he did so, and the parties were subsequently to reach a satisfactory interests-based settlement at mediation—one that did not provide simply for a monetary payment—the effect of the new procedure, in theoretical terms, would be to move the parties from "successful" (in the sense that agreements were often reached) rights negotiation at step 3 to successful interests negotiation at mediation. Although this should reduce some costs of negotiation—by producing better outcomes, less recurrence of disputes, less strain on the relationship—the increased and highly visible transaction costs associated with the use of a third-party mediator would probably discourage employers and unions from continuing with the new procedure.

Did these risks outweigh the potential gains of the procedure? Other industries' experience with grievance mediation was too limited to answer the question. No data existed on the effect of mediation on the settlement rate in earlier steps of the grievance procedure. No data existed comparing mediation and arbitration in terms of time, cost, or participants' satisfaction. No data existed on the long-range effects of grievance mediation, such as whether it would increase participants' ability to resolve grievances through negotiation in the earlier steps of the grievance procedure or whether it would improve the quality of the labor-management relationship. Accordingly, we decided to undertake an experiment in grievance mediation. Conducting such an experiment, however, would require funds to establish and administer a mediation system, collect evaluation data, and analyze those data. It would also require us to persuade coal companies and the UMWA to try a procedure with which they had no experience and that was little used elsewhere in American industry.

Becoming Involved

Negotiating to Obtain Funds and Participants

In the spring of 1980, we began discussing the proposed experiment with the U.S. Department of Labor's Labor-Management Services Administration, headed by William Hobgood. Hobgood, who had earlier helped Goldberg develop the mediation procedure, had learned about the coal industry's dispute problems from his work on contract negotiations when he was with the Federal Mediation and Conciliation Service. After considerable discussion, we received informal assurances that the Labor Department would probably fund a six-month experiment if we could persuade enough coal companies and union districts to participate.

We decided to begin the experiment in two union districts and to involve as many of the coal companies operating in those districts as possible. We would choose one district where relations were generally good, thus maximizing the prospects for successful mediation, and one district with less satisfactory relationships, to test mediation under difficult circumstances. We selected District 28 (southwestern Virginia) for its good relations and District 30 (eastern Kentucky) for its less satisfactory relations. Whereas District 28 was in the bottom quartile of the union in terms of its rate of arbitration and wildcat strikes, District 30 had high rates of both.

Despite the apparent advantages of the mediation proposal, we soon discovered many obstacles to its adoption. Prominent among these was inertia. Arbitration (supplemented by wildcat strikes) had been an accepted mode of dispute resolution in the coal industry for approximately seventy years; whatever its flaws, it was thoroughly known. Mediation, in contrast, was largely unknown, and the prospect was daunting for some union and company representatives. Closely associated with this was the fact that many company and union representatives were quite skilled at arbitration and were dubious about trying a procedure that called for different skills.

Another obstacle to the adoption of mediation (not fully recognized by us at the time) was that arbitration fits more easily into the bureaucratic structure of both union and management than does mediation. Arbitration has well-established rules and procedures. The outcome is predictable: the grievance will either be denied, sustained, or sustained in part. Precise records can be kept of both the results (the number of cases won and lost by each party) and the arbitrators (the number of cases each arbitrator decided for the union and for the company), which fits nicely with the bureaucratic penchant for record keeping. Mediation, in contrast, is a fluid procedure with few rules. The outcome is unpredictable, because the issue may expand or contract during mediation and because the range of possible settlements is great. Score keeping is difficult, because many grievances are resolved by compromise.

A further obstacle concerned control over the presentation of evidence and arguments. In arbitration, control is held firmly by union and company staff representatives; in mediation, where there are no procedural rules, their control is not nearly so tight. Although miners might welcome the prospect of greater control over their grievances, representatives might balk at surrendering a measure of power.[9]

Other obstacles also arose. Mediation, with its emphasis on compromise, was distasteful to those company and union representatives with a highly developed sense of right and wrong; they preferred arbitration, in which a third party decides who is right and who is wrong. Similarly, arbitration was preferable for those who wished a forum in which to test their strength against the opposition. In addition, some company and union representatives were reluctant because they thought that a settlement at mediation would be evidence of failure on their part; if the grievance could be settled, they should have been able to settle it without calling in a mediator. Some employers opposed mediation because they feared that its speed and low cost would encourage more frequent union challenges to management action.

Finally, lack of trust was a substantial barrier. Some employer representatives feared that the union would accept the new procedure only to obtain more advantageous settlements. Some union representatives feared that employers would accept the procedure only to add a step to the grievance process, thereby increasing the union's costs and the length of time to ultimate resolution. Each feared that the other might use information learned during mediation to prepare its arguments for arbitration.

Goldberg tried to overcome these objections. He assured both union and company representatives that the skills they used in attempting to settle grievances at step 3 were essentially the same skills they would use in mediation. To representatives who disliked the idea of compromise, he emphasized that, when no settlement could be reached, the mediator would tell the parties who was right and who was wrong. To employers who feared easy union access to mediation, he emphasized the mediator's lack of power to bind the company to any agreement it did not voluntarily accept. To everyone, Goldberg argued that whatever risks mediation entailed, they were minimal compared to those in the existing system. His central message, delivered at countless meetings with both management and union representatives, was this: "The existing system of grievance resolution in the coal industry is unsatisfactory. You are spending vast amounts of money on arbitration, and the enormous backlog of cases means that you do not get arbitrators' decisions for months. Neither the miners nor the companies benefit from this situation, because dissatisfied miners engage in frequent wildcat strikes that deprive them of wages and the companies of profits. Grievance mediation may not be the answer to this problem, but the risks of experimenting with it for a few months are minimal, while the potential gains, if it really works, are great. Not only will you save time and money, you may also develop improved settlement skills and a better relationship. Thus, you should give it a try."

The parties were swayed by different arguments. The union's primary interest turned out to be the potential savings in time and money. The employers' primary interest turned out to be the prospect of an improved relationship. As a result, both parties were willing to participate in the experiment, albeit for different reasons. Districts 28 and 30 both agreed to a six-month experiment, as did nearly all the companies in District 30 and two of the three large companies in District 28. Once we had achieved this level of participation, the Labor Department agreed to fund the experiment.

At the end of the first six months, Districts 28 and 30, and the participating companies in those districts, agreed to extend the experiment for another six months. Also accepting our invitation to join the experiment, after a similar series of meetings, were District 11 (Indiana) and District 12 (Illinois), along with one of the two large companies in District 11 and three companies in District 12.[10]

We were surprised at how much time and effort were required to get participants for the experiment. Easily twice as much time was spent in negotiating the acceptance of mediation as had been spent in developing it. Rolf Valtin, a former chief arbitrator under the contract between the union and the employers, consulted with us extensively and served as one of the initial mediators for the experiment. He subsequently wrote:

> The mediation of grievances in coal was an innovative idea. As is true of other institutions in a democracy, collective bargaining is not prone to welcome innovative ideas with open arms. To fly, they have to be pushed and sold. The mediation idea was no exception.
>
> Yes, Steve [Goldberg] sat down and wrote a proposal. And yes, Steve got encouragement from those of us with whom he shared the proposal, and from an interested Department of Labor, and even from some high officials at the national level of the Industry and the Union. But none of this was nearly enough to convert the idea to concrete action. What had to be produced was the acceptance of the idea on the part of those who would do the implementing—i.e., the field reps, the mine labor relations people, the mine committees, and the mine superintendents. These are tough people with practical concerns, and theirs is not a world which tends to side with an idea because of its nobility. Countless meetings had to be held: to overcome skepticism and plain resistance to change, to demonstrate that mediation might be worth taking a shot at, to alter or make adjustments in proposed ground rules, to deal with negativism based on fears that the other side had more to gain, etc. All of this translates to selling. Without it, there would be no mediation of grievances in coal. And without it, the

idea is not likely to take hold in other collective-bargaining arenas. The inherent strength of the idea is simply not enough.[11]

Putting the Changes into Place

Mediating the Rules and Training the Participants

Once Districts 28 and 30 and employers in those districts had agreed to join the mediation experiment, Goldberg met with them to work out the rules. We had by then developed a model set of mediation rules (set out in the Appendix to this book), which he presented to the parties. In general, the only rule that resulted in significant discussion and occasional disagreement dealt with sending grievances to mediation. The model rules provided that the consent of both parties was necessary, but we made it plain that the parties could, if they wished, instead adopt a rule by which one party could send a grievance to mediation without the consent of the other. The argument in favor of mutual consent is that if both parties agree to mediation, the likelihood of reaching a settlement should be greater than if one party does not want to mediate. The contrary argument is that if mutual consent is needed to mediate, mediation will rarely if ever take place—when unsuccessful premediation settlement negotiations result in hostility, mutual consent may be impossible. The parties in both Districts 28 and 30 began the experiment with a mutual consent requirement for sending grievances to mediation.

After six months, the District 28 parties agreed to mediate all grievances except discharge cases, which would continue to require mutual consent. The District 28 approach was also adopted by the parties in Districts 11 and 12.

Goldberg mediated occasional disagreements concerning such issues as how many union representatives could attend a mediation conference and who would pay them for any wages lost as a result of attending such a conference. On the whole, though, the proposed rules were adopted without significant change.

The next step was to meet jointly with the company and union personnel who were going to select grievances for mediation and present the grievances to the mediators. At each meeting, Goldberg explained the rules and the procedures to the participants, few of whom had ever engaged in mediation. He wanted to be certain that the participants understood the rules well, so that few disputes about their meaning would arise during mediation. He also emphasized that mediation focused not on rights—which party was "right" and which was "wrong" under the collective bargaining contract—but on interests. The goal would be to reach a negotiated settlement that satisfied the vital interests of each. Only if this proved impossible would the negotiations address contractual rights.

Goldberg tried to prepare the participants for their obligations at mediation. "You don't have to come to mediation prepared to surrender what you think are important rights," he said. "However, you do have to be prepared to listen with an open mind to what the other party says and what the mediator says. Furthermore, if the other side will accept a settlement that meets your interests, you should be prepared to accept that settlement." He told them that mediation would not always be easy: "At times, you are going to have to recognize that you don't have a very strong case, and the other side isn't offering much by way of settlement. In that situation, rather than go to arbitration, you may have to bite the bullet and accept a settlement that some of your people won't like." He also told them that their distrust was understandable but that it should not deter them from experimenting with mediation. "Don't just assume that the other side won't mediate in good faith. Test them in a case or two. The worst that can happen is that you will have wasted a few hundred dollars trying to get a settlement, but that's less than the cost of a single arbitration." Goldberg did not do any hands-on mediation training, because we did not have simulation materials; since then, we have developed such materials and conduct both a mediation demonstration and joint mediation training as part of familiarization meetings.

Goldberg also tried to motivate the participants. He told them that they would have opportunity for voice: "In mediation, you won't have to worry about legal rules of evidence. Everybody will get a chance to talk, and you can say what you want in your own way." He told them that the outcomes of mediation would be mutually satisfactory: "Unless both sides are satisfied, there's no agreement. Thus, any agreement that you do reach will be satisfactory to both of you." He also suggested that mediation should be easier on the relationship than arbitration: "Trying to work out an agreement you can both accept is less likely to lead to hard feelings than is trying to convince the arbitrator that you're right and the other side is wrong." Finally, he pointed to the low transaction costs of successful mediation and what that would mean to them: "If you approach mediation with a genuine desire to reach a satisfactory settlement, the chances are excellent that you will be successful in settling three-quarters of your cases. And if you can do that, think of all the money you can save on arbitration, which you will have available for other uses."

Selecting and Training the Mediators

We thought that the success of the mediation procedure would depend largely on the skill of the mediators. If they could not help the parties successfully negotiate settlements, the procedure would fail. As a result, we spent considerable effort in selecting third-party neutrals to recommend to the parties. Initially, we had to decide whether, in view of the hybrid nature of the grievance mediation procedure, the third parties should be experienced primarily in mediation or in arbitration (at the time, very few neutrals had substantial experience in both). There were strong arguments in favor of each alternative. Using experienced coal industry arbitrators known to the parties would motivate participation in grievance mediation. It would also enhance the disputants' confidence in the third party and make the advisory opinion more persuasive. Finally, it would increase the likelihood that the advisory opinion would prove accurate if the grievance ultimately went to arbitration. At the same time, using third parties with mediation experience would more effectively bring about settlements through interests-based negotiation, and it would help train the participants in negotiation techniques. We resolved this dilemma for the first round of mediator selection by a compromise: our primary selection criterion would be arbitration experience, but preference would be given to those experienced arbitrators who also had mediation experience.

Our next decision was whether to limit our selection to those mediators who were generally regarded as the coal industry's leading arbitrators. The argument for choosing widely known arbitrators was similar to that for choosing arbitrators over mediators—to encourage participation and increase confidence in the advisory opinion. The risk was that we might not discover a possible weakness in the procedure. If the procedure succeeded only when the third party was recognized as an expert in contract interpretation, its capacity for diffusion would diminish significantly. We would not know whether this was so if our experimental group of third parties consisted only of recognized experts. As powerful as the latter argument was, it did not prevail. We decided that it would be difficult enough to resolve disputes between hostile parties who had a history of turbulent labor relations and no mediation experience, and that we should do all in our power to make the experiment work in its early stages. If it survived that period, there would be ample time to experiment with less well-known third parties. Indeed, if grievance mediation was successful, the limited number of recognized experts would compel such a change.

We wanted all mediators to have a substantial case load, so we decided to recommend only four mediators for the initial two-district experiment. Three of the four mediators were accepted. The fourth was accused of having a pro-management bias by some District 30 locals, and District 30 took the position that unless he were removed from the list of mediators, it would not participate in the experiment. He was removed, a substitute was nominated and approved, and the experiment remained alive in District 30. The four mediators in the initial experiment were James Scearce, David Beckman, Valtin, and Goldberg. When the experiment was expanded to Districts 11 and 12, we added Thomas Phelan and Anthony Sinicropi. Each of the mediators had substantial arbitration experience, in coal and other industries, and four of the six had extensive mediation experience as well.

We met with the mediators before the experiment began. We briefly discussed the rules of mediation, but our primary message was that the mediator must prod the parties to engage in interests-based negotiation, rather than allowing them to treat the procedure as rights-based advisory arbitration.

Grievance Mediation Begins

The first grievance mediation in the history of the coal industry took place on November 3, 1980, in Castlewood, Virginia. The parties were District 28 and Clinchfield Coal Company. The local union was protesting the company's having contracted out repair work on mine machinery to another employer, arguably depriving Clinchfield employees of that work. The discussion was wide-ranging, focusing both on the contractual rights of the parties and on alternatives that would meet the interests of both company and union. Several settlement proposals were made and discussed, and the parties worked hard to reach a settlement. Ultimately, however, no settlement was reached, so the mediator, David Beckman, gave his advisory decision: the grievance would be denied. The union chose not to accept the advisory decision, instead taking the grievance to arbitration—where, contrary to the prediction, it was sustained a few months later.

It seemed that the first mediation had been a total disaster. Not only had the parties failed to reach a settlement, but the mediator's advisory opinion had differed from the arbitrator's actual decision. With some trepidation, Goldberg telephoned representatives of both parties to determine their reaction. Both stated that they thought the procedure had worked well and were willing to try it again. Additionally, the union representative admitted that he had been surprised by the arbitrator's decision and thought that most arbitrators would have decided the grievance as the mediator had predicted. Thus, the experiment's start had not been as bad as we had initially feared.

Subsequently, the mediation process began to function as we hoped it would. Reporter James Warren, writing in the *Chicago Tribune*, described one mediation session:

> An angry coal miner is perhaps the closest thing the nation has to a two-legged nuclear weapon, and, on a recent day, Doc Wellington was one unhappy miner. His rage was forming on one of those sunny, cloudless days that seem to accent the lush and tranquil greens of coal country, but whose peacefulness belies the dirty and often deadly jobs that people perform in the ground below.
>
> After parking a tractor, the bearded Wellington ambled up a driveway and into the office of his employer. He was there strenuously objecting that a less senior miner had leapfrogged him, getting lucrative vacation work that allowed him to work and be paid overtime while the mine was shut down for a period. Sitting three shotgun lengths from a group including Bob Gossman, the labor relations director, Wellington declared, "This was all Gossman's screw-up!"
>
> Was the violence notorious in the coal fields about to erupt at the Wabash mine of Amax Coal Co.? Contrary to appearances, no. Both Wellington and Gossman actually were involved in grievance mediation. . . .
>
> The accent is on the informal, as evidenced with Doc Wellington. An Amax supervisor had thought only two members of Wellington's day

shift would be needed for vacation work. He thus
asked Wellington only if he would be interested
in vacation work on the two later shifts. Wellington, a proud fellow who prefers his day shift,
said no.

Just before the vacation, the company
posted a third vacancy for the day shift on a bulletin board, but no one told Wellington about it,
and the job was taken by a less senior worker
who had previously agreed to work a later shift.

Amax contended that by declining to work
the later two shifts, Doc had effectively said he
didn't want to work at all. The company admitted it hadn't specifically notified him of its later
need for a third worker on the day shift but said
Wellington should have read the bulletin board.

Wearing slacks and a sports shirt, the mediator sat Wellington down at a table with union
and company officials and asked everybody to
begin explaining their positions. There was no
witness box or stenographer. It was all very con-
versational and loose.

Puffing on a cigarette, Doc Wellington
said: "The only gripe I have is why I wasn't
asked to work my own shift. Bob Gossman's
right, I turned down the second and third shift.
But that's because I don't think I should work
those."

The mediator asked management to leave
and probed deeper with the union, seeking to
learn how one might avoid such a future snafu.
He then told the union to leave, brought back
management and delicately suggested that he was
troubled by the fact that Wellington had never
been directly asked about work on his own shift.

"Quite candidly, I think you have a loser if
this goes to arbitration," said the mediator, also
an experienced arbitrator.

He thus utilized a critical element of the method; the potential pressure in suggesting what end a costly arbitration might bring. It is a pressure point born of labor contracts and thus not really transferrable to nonunion firms without real grievance procedures.

If Amax lost an arbitration, it might have to pay Doc about $1,800 for 17 shifts of pay he arguably missed during the vacation period (including triple time on a Sunday). Gossman reiterated that "I've got a real problem with a guy turning down work and then getting any money."

The mediator patiently continued and, along the way, got the union to admit that any foul-up was surely inadvertent. He pointed out the union also had a weak point if the case went to arbitration: Wellington's failure to look at the bulletin board.

Over two hours, both sides slowly moved far from rigid stances, and a deal was struck. Doc would get paid for nine shifts, or about $1,000, and procedures would be improved for future vacation openings.

Union official Rick Tygett estimated that by avoiding arbitration, he saved as much as $2,000, including the payment of lost wages for some hearing witnesses. Gossman and mine manager Steve Garcia figured they saved perhaps $1,500. Instead, the two sides split the mediator's daily fee of $600, which he gets regardless of how many grievances he handles (there were two this day).

But there was something more important than money. "You aren't left with a bad taste in your mouth after mediation," Garcia said. "Arbitration is a semi-hostile environment, a win-lose situation. This lets a guy blow off steam right in front of you."

"There are a lot of labor-relations people who carry arbitration won-lost records tattooed on their arms," Gossman said, "but maintaining rapport with your people is important." He noted with pride that even with 739 hourly employees, not one grievance had gone to arbitration in three years.

"With mediation, you get a settlement both agree to, not just what a third-party says," Tygett said. "And even after you win arbitrations, bad feelings remain. I'd grade this an A-plus."[12]

Calibration

In the early days of grievance mediation, Goldberg closely monitored the procedure, so that he could make any changes necessary to aid its smooth functioning. He mediated regularly in all the experimental districts, observing and sometimes commenting on the negotiating skills of the participants. He talked with participants about their reactions, criticisms, and suggestions. He had similar discussions by telephone with those union and company representatives whom he had not recently seen in mediation, and tried to encourage their use of the process.

Goldberg also held feedback meetings in each district every six months for the first two years. At these meetings, he and Brett provided the participants with a statistical report that covered the preceding six months. This report generally showed a high settlement rate, along with substantial cost savings. These results helped motivate the parties to continue using mediation. The participants also used these meetings to discuss problems that had developed in the preceding six months. For example, the parties in District 28 were concerned that mediation was not being used sufficiently. After extensive discussion at a feedback meeting, they adopted a rule providing that no grievances (except those involving discharges) could go to arbitration unless the parties had first tried mediation. Another problem that sometimes arose at the meetings was performance of the mediators. When a particular mediator was identified as unsatisfactory, he would either receive suggestions for improvement (transmitted through Goldberg) or be replaced.

We also held feedback meetings with the mediators. These meetings served as a forum for discussing problems, an opportunity for developing mediation techniques, and a means of reinforcing a sense of mission among the mediators. Goldberg kept in touch with the mediators in other ways as well. He telephoned each new mediator after his first day of mediation to discuss his experiences, answer his questions, and in the absence of a settlement, to provide reassurance. Goldberg also wrote or telephoned each mediator who reported a particularly creative settlement, both to discuss the settlement and to praise the mediator.[13]

Evaluating the Results

Results of the Experiment

The experiment was a success in every respect. Twenty-three of the 25 mediation conferences held in the first six months resulted in settlements, as did 136 of 153 (89 percent) of those held in the first twelve months. Fifty-one percent of the settlements were compromises; in 15 percent, the union withdrew the grievance; and in 7 percent, the company granted the grievance.[14]

At the end of the first twelve-month period, we surveyed participant satisfaction. We questioned five groups of people with experience with both mediation and arbitration—company labor relations representatives, union district representatives, company operating personnel, local union officers, and grievants. A substantial majority of all groups preferred mediation to arbitration. This was particularly so at the mine level, where company operating personnel preferred mediation by six to one and union officers did so by seven to one.

We found that mediation did not cause earlier steps in the grievance procedure to be treated as pro forma. The parties did not mediate cases they would otherwise have settled in earlier steps of the grievance procedure, but only cases that would otherwise have been taken to arbitration. Thus, settlement rates at step 3 did not diminish significantly after the introduction of mediation. The one exception was District 28, where, during the second six months of the experiment, some grievances were taken to mediation that would otherwise have been settled at step 3. Thereafter, however, the step 3 settlement rate in District 28 returned to its pre-experiment level, and it has remained at that level or higher ever since.[15]

The cost and time savings of mediation were substantial. The average cost per mediation case was $295 (mediator's fee and expenses), less than one-third of the average cost of arbitration. (The average cost of arbitration—arbitrator's fee and expenses—in the experimental districts during the experimental period was $1,034 per case.) The average time between the request for mediation and the mediation conference (at which nearly all grievances were resolved) was 15 days; the average time between the request for arbitration and the issuance of the arbitrator's decision was 109 days.

No grievant sued the union, during the experimental period or afterward, for breaching its duty of fair representation by not taking a grievance from mediation to arbitration. In fact, in a number of cases, a duty of fair representation suit was pending when mediation took place, and the resolution reached at mediation included a settlement of the suit. In some of those cases, the mediation gave the grievant a better settlement than had previously been offered. In others, though no better settlement was offered, the grievant was willing to drop both his claim and his suit after presenting his claim to a respected neutral and hearing the neutral's opinion that his claim was without merit.

We cannot be certain whether the first twelve months of mediation stimulated the participants to use interests negotiation in other interactions or improved their overall relationship. The parties had been dealing with each other in an adversarial fashion for many years before the advent of mediation, and the experience of individual company and union personnel with mediation in the first twelve months was limited. Except for the company labor relations representatives and the union district representatives, nobody participated in mediation more than five times during this period. If changes in dispute-handling procedures or overall relationships can be brought about by experience with problem-solving negotiations in mediation, it may be that more experience than this is necessary.

The years since may have provided the necessary experience. In early 1986, when mediation had been in use for approximately six years, we conducted a survey of the participants. Some, albeit not all, believed that, over time, mediation had affected the dispute resolution skills of both union and management representatives. One union district president said, "Now, they look for solutions to problems instead of stonewalling. Attitudes have been expanded, [they are] not as close-minded as they used to be, even at step 2 and step 3." A company labor relations director reported, "At one mine, both the superintendent and the mine committee reported to me, following a few successful mediation hearings, that they would not be back to mediation. If they could work out their problems that well with others observing, they could do just as well at the mine. They kept that commitment." Mediation also had effects outside the grievance resolution procedure. According to some participants, the relationship between union and management at some mines became more cooperative and less aggressive. "Mediation," said one union representative, "shows that things can be talked out and settled, even if not always."

The effect of mediation on the frequency of wildcat strikes is unclear. Although wildcat strikes have decreased where mediation is used, they have also decreased by approximately the same amount where mediation is not used. The reduction is generally attributed to improved labor relations, difficult economic times, and reduced employment in the industry. Some mediation participants said that the prompt availability of mediation and its capacity to achieve mutually acceptable outcomes directly prevented threatened strikes. Far more participants commented that mediation indirectly deterred strikes by improving communication between management and the union.

Limits on the Effectiveness of Grievance Mediation

We found that, contrary to our fears, the mediation procedure functioned effectively with third parties who were not experienced arbitrators. At our request, disputants used mediators who had less arbitration experience than the original six but who did have substantial mediation experience. Those mediators used their mediation expertise to help the parties reach interests-based settlements without using an advisory opinion. Thus, their settlement rate was as high as that of the original mediators.

We also found that while the quality of the overall relationship between the union and the company was not important in obtaining settlements, the relationship between the representatives of the company and the union was quite important. If they dealt with each other in a good-faith effort, they could obtain settlements despite a hostile relationship between the parties they represented. However, this point must be qualified. Where the union-management relationship is generally poor, the company and the union will probably abandon mediation. The representatives of the parties may make agreements, but the parties themselves must carry them out; where the relationship is bad, agreements are frequently not carried out in a mutually satisfactory manner. When that happens, one or both parties may lose interest in a procedure directed toward agreement. For this reason, individual mines, and in some cases entire companies, have ceased mediating.

Reasons for the Success of Grievance Mediation

In order to improve and diffuse the practice of grievance mediation, we needed to know not just that the experiment succeeded but also why. Part of the answer is that the representatives relied on the mediator's opinion about the merits of the grievance to discourage their own side from continuing on to arbitration. For example, many mediators had the following experience: In the course of a private meeting with the union, the union representative would ask the mediator for an advisory opinion. The mediator would reply that the union had very little chance of prevailing. The union representative would turn to the grievant and say, "That's what I've been trying to tell you." At that point, the grievance would be either dropped or, with the grievant's expectations lowered, quickly resolved.

A second factor that helped create the success was that the parties were willing to discuss grievances almost entirely in terms of their respective interests, with little, if any, reference to the contract. In some cases, mediators told us, discussion centered almost entirely on the question of whether the company had treated the grievant fairly. The participants placed particular emphasis on this point. In our initial survey, the reason that participants most often gave for the success of mediation was its interests-centered approach. For example, one company representative said, "I like the informality. It creates an atmosphere of people trying to solve problems through talk, rather than being enemies in a legal process. This is a much better way to approach these problems." Participants made similar comments in the 1986 survey. They agreed that mediation was superior to arbitration in dealing with grievances that were symptomatic of an underlying problem. One union representative said, "That's one of the best aspects of it. You get at the gripes as well as the grievances." Another union representative stated, "I feel about 70 percent of all the grievances I handle have an underlying problem. Arbitration never has a chance dealing with that type of situation. Mediation does." A company labor relations director added, "Mediation definitely brings out the personality conflicts and addresses them, while arbitration never deals with them."

A third factor was satisfaction with outcomes. Most of the participants said that mediation leads to more satisfactory outcomes than does arbitration. The reason, they said, was partly that in mediation "both sides go behind the charge to what's really on their minds" (company labor relations consultant) and partly that the outcome is crafted by the participants, not by a third party. "We have more impact on the settlement, and how it's worded. There's no difficult legal language like in arbitration rulings" (union representative). A company labor relations director also pointed out, "The satisfaction of reaching a settlement raises both parties' confidence level in the grievance procedure."

Finally, mediation enhanced the participants' voice and control. The mediators reported that the grievant and local union officers, freed from the procedural constraints and evidentiary rules of arbitration, played a greater role and exercised more control over the treatment of their grievances than was typical in arbitration. Participants also said that compliance with mediation settlements was generally easier to obtain than was compliance with arbitration awards. This was partly because the parties were more likely to understand a settlement that they had helped draft and partly because they had agreed to comply with it. "Mediation is something agreed to, versus 'Ha-ha, I beat you!' We'll do as little as we can to comply with arbitration decisions" (company labor relations consultant). "In mediation, there is a strong sense of being bound, so both parties do it" (mine labor relations director).

Despite the overall success of the method, a few participants voiced criticisms. Some company representatives complained that at times the mediators appeared to be pushing them toward a settlement that they did not want. One company representative said, "Upper management wants more from the union, while the mediators keep asking for more from the company." Other comments by employer representatives were that "Mediators shouldn't try to force settlement if one side or the other really doesn't want to" and "It seems as if the mediators want a settlement at any cost regardless of the contract." This criticism, which is also heard in contract negotiation mediation, is probably inevitable. A mediator's settlement rate is the only tangible measure of his ability, so the mediator is apt to become quite ego involved in his efforts to achieve a settlement. From a party's perspective, however, an unsatisfactory settlement may be worse than no settlement. Hence, the tension. And the mediator's pressure may seem to fall disproportionately on the company, because many settlements require the company to give something to the union. The problem tends to diminish, however, as the parties become more familiar with mediation and develop the capacity to resist mediator pressure.

Continued Use of Mediation

Of the participants in the original experiment, all of the districts and a majority of the companies have retained the mediation procedure, though its use has been sporadic in District 30. When it is used, mediation has remained successful in resolving grievances short of arbitration. As of June 1988, 827 coal industry grievances had been mediated; only 20 percent went on to arbitration. The cost and time savings of mediation have also continued to be great. The average cost of mediation in the period from November 1980 to June 1988 was $330 per case, less than 20 percent of the average cost of arbitration ($1,692).[16] The time from the request for mediation to final resolution in the same period was twenty-four days; no comparable figure for arbitration is available for that period, but there is no reason to suppose that it was significantly less than the 109-day average of 1980–81.

Two of the major companies that participated in the 1981–82 experiment subsequently withdrew, one in 1983, the other in 1984. In one case, the company's chief operating officer thought that because mediation was less expensive and faster than arbitration, the union was using it to interfere with his freedom to manage the company.[17] In the other case, company labor relations personnel believed that a union representative who was running for reelection was taking unreasonable positions in mediation, such as refusing to drop weak cases, for fear of alienating union members. As a result, grievances either were not settled or were settled on terms that the company regarded as unfavorable.[18]

Exit

One of our objectives has been to transform mediation from a procedure that was brought into the coal industry by Goldberg and that was associated with him into a procedure that belongs to the participants, that they use because they find it desirable, and that they will continue to use after we have turned our attention elsewhere. To this end, Goldberg no longer mediates, and we phased out our feedback meetings in all except one district. Some evidence indicates that these efforts have been successful. Considerable change has taken place in the leadership positions of the union districts and companies that began mediation in 1980; few of those with whom Goldberg originally dealt remain in charge of their organizations. Mediation has survived those changes, which is one sign that it has become institutionalized as part of the dispute resolution structure.

While we have sought to minimize our presence, we have continued to provide resources necessary for the efficient operation of mediation. In 1983, we formed a not-for-profit corporation, Mediation Research and Education Project, Inc., to handle the administrative details of mediation.[19] The MREP office receives requests for mediation, assigns mediators in response to requests, and collects and analyzes data for evaluating the effectiveness of mediation.

Diffusion

Diffusion Within the Coal Industry

Our initial goal was to change the dispute resolution system in the entire coal industry by encouraging the adoption of grievance mediation on an industrywide basis. We have continued our efforts to achieve that goal. Valtin, Hobgood, and Goldberg have described the mediation procedure and its results publicly at coal industry conferences and privately to union and company officials. We have also had company and union participants in mediation describe their experiences, both in joint union-management meetings and in separate meetings of each. Finally, we have urged people considering mediation to observe actual mediation sessions, and a number have done so.

These efforts have met with mixed results. On the positive side, mediation was expressly authorized by both the 1984 and 1988 national collective bargaining contracts between the UMWA and the coal companies. This resulted in the adoption of mediation by some union locals in the experimental districts that had previously held back out of a sense that any procedure not in the contract was suspect. Still, until recently, mediation had been little used outside the four experimental districts. In 1982–84, approximately twenty-five cases were mediated in Districts 17 and 29 (both in West Virginia). Twenty of those twenty-five cases were settled, but for reasons not clear to us, mediation did not become an accepted part of the grievance procedure in either district. In 1986, District 5 (Pennsylvania) and Beth Energy Coal Company began mediating grievances. In 1987–88, mediation agreements were entered into between District 20 (Alabama) and three major companies in that district. Thus, of twenty-two UMWA districts, mediation has been used in eight.

Diffusion Outside the Coal Industry

Although the coal industry's rate of arbitration in the 1970s was the highest of all industries in the United States, some other industries and several individual employer-union relationships have an arbitration rate that seems higher than necessary. The railroad industry and the U.S. Postal Service, for example, are both thought to have needlessly high ratios of arbitration to negotiated grievance settlements.[20] Even where arbitration is not used excessively, it is often criticized as inefficient. Complaints about the high cost, delays, and excessive formality of arbitration are staples of the industrial relations literature, and have been for many years.[21]

We believed that grievance mediation might help other industries by encouraging employers and unions to reduce their dependence on rights-based arbitration in favor of a more interests-based approach. Beginning in 1982, we sought to interest other industries in experimenting with mediation. These efforts have been reasonably successful. Grievance mediation has spread to a number of industries, including manufacturing, telephone, urban mass transit, retail sales, petroleum refining, electric power, local government, and public education.

Our role in getting mediation started in these industries has varied considerably. At one extreme, employers and unions, stimulated by our speeches or writings but with no direct contact with us, have negotiated their own grievance mediation procedure. This type of diffusion is clearly the most efficient. It also maximizes the prospects for institutionalization of mediation, since ownership of the process rests with the parties from the very beginning. In other cases, an employer or union has asked us for a model contract clause, a set of rules for mediation, and suggestions on how to begin mediating. After that, they have designed and administered their own procedure with no further involvement by us. At the other extreme, in some relationships we have played nearly as substantial a role as we did in the coal industry. At the invitation of one or both parties, we have worked as systems designers, establishing rules and procedures.

Frequently, the parties have adapted our model to fit their relationship. For example, in one relationship, attorneys were regularly used for arbitration, and the parties expected to use them in mediation. The parties feared that the attorneys would focus too much on obtaining a favorable advisory decision and too little on searching for an outcome that satisfied the interests of each, turning mediation into a rights-dominated procedure, so they decided to dispense with the advisory opinion. In another relationship, the parties anticipated that they would need mediation in few cases but that those cases would be extremely important. They agreed to use one mediator, who would become thoroughly familiar with their needs and concerns, for all cases.

One barrier to our efforts to spread grievance mediation beyond the coal industry has been the opposition of some lawyers. This opposition has been based partly on the belief that grievance mediation would not be in a particular client's best interest, but other factors have also contributed. Until recently, few law schools taught anything about mediation. Many lawyers do not understand the process and have had no experience with it. As a result, they tend to be dubious about advising a client to try it. Additionally, many labor lawyers derive a substantial portion of their income from representing companies or unions in arbitration. Grievance mediation, in which the parties are rarely represented by lawyers, poses a threat to that income.[22]

Where mediation has been adopted in other industries, the results have been essentially the same as those in the coal industry. Between May 1983 and June 1988, 276 grievances went to mediation in industries other than coal, of which 81 percent were resolved without resort to arbitration. The average cost of mediation (mediator's fees and expenses) has been $435 per case, approximately 30 percent of the average cost of arbitration. The average time from the request for mediation to the final resolution has been 26 days, approximately 10 percent of the comparable average for arbitration.[23]

Conclusion

Our initial objective was to reduce the use of high-cost arbitration in the coal industry by encouraging interests-based mediation. Where mediation has been adopted, that objective has been substantially met. The problem has been diffusion within the coal industry. Since 1981, grievance mediation has spread more widely outside the coal industry than within it.

An obvious question is whether mediation would have spread more rapidly in the coal industry if we had involved representatives of the parties in the diagnosis and design stages. This might well have made a difference. In other industries, when the parties have been involved in establishing mediation, they have been active in its diffusion. Thus, our own experience with grievance mediation serves to underline the importance of involving the parties in the systems design effort from the start.

Still, the future looks bright. An increasing number of companies and unions are adopting grievance mediation on their own initiative, without substantial involvement by us, other than as catalysts, spreading the idea. They are achieving great success with the procedure, resolving grievances satisfactorily, quickly, and at low cost. As more companies and unions learn of this success, we anticipate still further use of grievance mediation.

Chapter 8

❖❖❖

Conclusion
The Promise of Dispute Systems Design

In conclusion, five points:

The Framework: Interests, Rights, and Power

This book offers a simple framework for understanding the process of dispute resolution. Three major ways to resolve a dispute are to reconcile underlying interests, to determine who is right, and to determine who has more power. This framework allows us not only to classify such disparate dispute resolution procedures as negotiation, adjudication, and strikes but also to understand how they interrelate.

Our basic proposition is that, in general, it is less costly and more rewarding to focus on interests than to focus on rights, which in turn is less costly and more rewarding than to focus on power. The straightforward prescription that follows is to encourage the parties to resolve disputes by reconciling their interests wherever it is possible and, where it is not, to use low-cost methods to determine rights and power.

One strength of this framework is that, in a few parsimonious concepts, it captures a great deal of what people do to improve the process of dispute resolution. Much current negotiation advice aims at replacing traditional bargaining

169

over rigid positions, where the focus is power, with problem-solving negotiation, where the focus is on creatively reconciling interests. Similarly, much of the effort of the alternative dispute resolution movement is aimed at replacing rights procedures such as litigation with interests-based procedures such as problem-solving negotiation and mediation.

The framework also applies beyond the kinds of dispute resolution systems covered in this book. One example at the societal level of a shift from a focus on power to a focus on rights is the replacement of the violent resolution of disputes with the rule of law, a process that is quite advanced within most nations but is still in its infancy among nations. Similarly, the democratic system can be understood as an attempt to replace high-cost power contests, such as coups d'etat and revolutions, with lower-cost contests, such as regular elections and parliamentary struggles. Elections not only lower the cost of determining power but also focus attention on people's interests.[1] The framework can thus provide insight into large-scale efforts to cut the costs of conflict.

The Goal: Savings and Gains

This book is about how to reduce the costs of resolving disputes: the hours wasted in futile quarreling, the ruinous expenses of lawsuits and strikes, and the strain on valued relationships. In organizations, these costs translate into losses in productivity and performance. In personal relationships, they translate into dissatisfaction and tension. At the extreme, the costs that designers seek to avoid are divorce, plant closings, injuries to life and limb, and the senseless destruction of war.

This book is also about gains: getting the most out of disputes. Conflict is a normal aspect of any relationship or organization. Resolving disputes effectively allows people and organizations to grow and change. The resolutions can result in mutual benefit, not only for the immediate disputants but for others who are affected by the same problem. Difficult trade-offs are faced and decisions made. Tensions are released and relationships strengthened. Productivity and performance are enhanced.

The Means: Dispute Systems Design

This book presents a practical method for achieving savings and gains. Any relationship or organization could benefit from a periodic dispute resolution diagnosis: a review of what kinds of disputes are occurring, how they are being resolved, and why some procedures are being used rather than others. Where the diagnosis indicates room for improvement, dispute systems design is in order: adding or altering procedures, strengthening motivation to use them, building skills, and adding resources. The great advantage of a systems approach is that it addresses not just a single dispute but the ongoing series of disputes that occur in any organization or relationship.

Such an exercise is best done even before the relationship or organization is formed. Anyone sitting down to work out a contract—lawyers with their clients, union representatives with management officials, diplomats negotiating a treaty—should consider establishing in advance an interests-based system for resolving disputes.

In this book, we set out six basic principles for designing an effective dispute resolution system. The first and most central is to put the focus on interests by encouraging the use of interests-based negotiation and mediation. The second is to provide rights and power "loop-backs"—procedures that turn the disputants' attention back to negotiation. The third principle is to provide rights and power "backups"—low-cost means for resolution if interests-based procedures fail. The fourth design principle—prevention—is to build in consultation to head off disputes before they arise and post-dispute feedback to prevent similar disputes in the future. The fifth principle is to arrange all these procedures in a low-to-high-cost sequence. And the final principle is to provide the motivation, skills, and resources necessary to make all the procedures work. Taken together, these six design principles form an integrated strategy for cutting the costs and achieving the potential gains of conflict.

An Application: Managing Intractable Conflicts and Preventing War

The field of conflict resolution is often criticized as being utopian. With some justification, the critics say that real conflicts of interest, such as those between labor and management or between Arabs and Israelis, cannot be solved: they are intractable. Dispute systems design offers a practical response. It does not aim to eliminate conflict but simply to resolve at low cost the resulting disputes.

Dispute systems design is similarly useful for preventing disputes from escalating into war or its equivalent. An old Ethiopian proverb holds: "When spider webs unite, they can halt a lion." A good dispute resolution system consists of a series of successive safety nets—negotiation followed by mediation, advisory arbitration, arbitration, third-party intervention, and so on—that can ensnare a dangerous conflict before it can do irreparable harm. An attempt is made to catch disputes early. If one procedure fails, another is waiting.

An effective dispute resolution system offers a way to accomplish the essential functions of violence and war, but at a significantly lower cost. The ultimate challenge is to devise workable dispute resolution systems not only for families and organizations but also for relations among nations. In an increasingly interdependent and insecure world, our survival depends on finding better means of resolving our differences than resorting to the ultimate power contest—nuclear war.

An Emerging Field

This book is a first step. Dispute systems design needs to be developed in both theory and practice. As a field, it is now in its infancy. In the future, dispute systems design may join the ranks of other well-known dispute resolution methods, such as mediation and arbitration. For some, it may one day become a profession. For many—managers, lawyers, diplomats, and others—it should become, just as negotiation is now, an essential tool in their repertoire of skills.

Appendix

Model Rules for Grievance Mediation in the Coal Industry (1980)

1. Mediation of a grievance will be scheduled only on the basis of a joint request for mediation by union and company representatives.
2. A request for mediation must be made within five calendar days of the step 3 meeting.
3. Mediation conferences will take place at a central location within the union district.
4. The grievant shall have the right to be present at the mediation conference.
5. Each party shall have one representative present its position to the mediator.
6. The representatives of the parties are encouraged, but not required, to present the mediator with a brief written statement of the facts, the issue, and the arguments in support of their position. If such a statement is not presented in written form, it shall be presented orally at the beginning of the mediation conference.
7. Any written material that is presented to the mediator shall be returned to the party presenting that material at the termination of the mediation conference.
8. Proceedings before the mediator shall be informal in

nature. The presentation of evidence is not limited to that presented at step 2 or 3 of the grievance proceedings, the rules of evidence will not apply, and no record of the mediation conference shall be made.

9. The mediator will have the authority to meet separately with any person or persons, but will not have the authority to compel the resolution of a grievance.

10. If no settlement is reached during the mediation conference, the mediator shall provide the parties with an immediate oral advisory decision, unless both parties agree that no decision shall be provided.

11. The mediator shall state the grounds of his or her advisory decision.

12. The advisory decision of the mediator, if accepted by the parties, shall not constitute a precedent, unless the parties otherwise agree.

13. If no settlement is reached at mediation, the parties are free to arbitrate. If they do so, arbitration must be requested within ten calendar days of the mediation conference.

14. In the event that a grievance that has been mediated subsequently goes to arbitration, no mediator may serve as arbitrator. Nothing said or done by the mediator may be referred to at arbitration. Nothing said or done by either party in the mediation conference may be used against it at arbitration.

15. The mediator shall conduct no more than three mediation conferences per day. Each mediation conference shall last no more than two and one-half hours.

16. The mediator's fee will be $150 per mediation conference, plus one-third of his or her expenses. The fee and expenses will be shared equally by the parties.

17. In the event that the mediation of a grievance is scheduled and then postponed or cancelled, the parties shall remain liable for the amounts specified in Rule 16 if no other grievance is substituted for that grievance postponed or cancelled.

Notes

Preface

1. See Kochan, T. A., Katz, H. C., and McKersie, R. B. *The Transformation of American Industrial Relations.* New York: Basic Books, 1986, pp. 91–93.

2. For a description of the International Harvester program, see McKersie, R. B., and Shropshire, W. W. "Avoiding Written Grievances: A Successful Program." *Journal of Business,* 1962, *35,* 135–152.

3. See *International Business Machines Corporation* v. *Fujitsu Limited,* American Arbitration Association, Commercial Arbitration Tribunal, Case no. 13-I-117-0636-85 (Sept. 15, 1987).

4. Davis, A. M. "Dispute Resolution at an Early Age." *Negotiation Journal,* 1986, *2,* 287–298.

5. Merry, S. E. "The Culture and Practice of Mediation in Parent-Child Conflicts." *Negotiation Journal,* 1987, *3,* 411–422.

6. The name Caney Creek is a pseudonym.

Chapter One

1. In order to steer between the Scylla of sexist language and the Charybdis of awkward writing, we have chosen to alternate the use of masculine and feminine pronouns.

2. This definition is taken from Felstiner, W.L.F., Abel, R. L., and Sarat, A. "The Emergence and Transformation of Disputes: Naming, Blaming, Claiming." *Law and Society Review*, 1980–81, *15*, 631–654. The article contains an interesting discussion of disputes and how they emerge.

3. See Felstiner, W.L.F., Abel, R. L., and Sarat, A. "The Emergence and Transformation of Disputes: Naming, Blaming, Claiming." *Law and Society Review*, 1980–81, *15*, 631–654.

4. In speaking of resolving disputes, rather than processing, managing, or handling disputes, we do not suggest that resolution will necessarily bring an end to the fundamental conflict underlying the dispute. Nor do we mean that a dispute once resolved will stay resolved. Indeed, one of our criteria for contrasting approaches to dispute resolution is the frequency with which disputes recur after they appear to have been resolved. See Merry, S. E., "Disputing Without Culture." *Harvard Law Review*, 1987, *100*, 2057–2073; Sarat, A. "The 'New Formalism' in Disputing and Dispute Processing." *Law and Society Review*, 1988, *21*, 695–715.

5. For an extensive discussion of interests-based negotiation, see Fisher, R., and Ury, W. L. *Getting to Yes.* Boston: Houghton Mifflin, 1981. See also Lax, D. A., and Sebenius, J. K. *The Manager as a Negotiator.* New York: Free Press, 1986.

6. Goldberg, S. B., and Sander, F.E.A. "Saying You're Sorry." *Negotiation Journal*, 1987, *3*, 221–224.

7. We recognize that in defining rights to include both legal entitlements and generally accepted standards of fairness, we are stretching that term beyond its commonly understood meaning. Our reason for doing so is that a procedure that uses either legal entitlements or generally accepted standards of fairness as a basis for dispute resolution will focus on the disputants' entitlements under normative standards, rather than on their underlying interests. This is true of adjudication, which deals with legal rights; it is equally true of rights-based negotiation, which may deal with either legal rights or generally accepted standards. Since, as we shall show, procedures that focus on normative standards are more costly than

those that focus on interests, and since our central concern is with cutting costs as well as realizing benefits, we find it useful to cluster together legal rights and other normative standards, as well as procedures based on either.

8. A court procedure may determine not only who is right but also who is more powerful, since behind a court decision lies the coercive power of the state. Legal rights have power behind them. Still, we consider adjudication a rights procedure, since its overt focus is determining who is right, not who is more powerful. Even though rights, particularly legal rights, do provide power, a procedure that focuses on rights as a means of dispute resolution is less costly than a procedure that focuses on power. A rights-based contest, such as adjudication, which focuses on which disputant ought to prevail under normative standards, will be less costly than a power-based strike, boycott, or war, which focuses on which disputant can hurt the other more. Similarly, a negotiation that focuses on normative criteria for dispute resolution will be less costly than a negotiation that focuses on the disputants' relative capacity to injure each other. Hence, from our cost perspective, it is appropriate to distinguish procedures that focus on rights from those that focus on power.

9. Emerson, R. M. "Power-Dependence Relations." *American Sociological Review,* 1962, *27,* 31–41.

10. Hirschman, A. O. *Exit, Voice, and Loyalty: Responses to Declines in Firms, Organizations and States.* Cambridge, Mass.: Harvard University Press, 1970. Exit corresponds with avoidance, loyalty with lumping it. Voice, as we shall discuss later, is most likely to be realized in interests-based procedures such as problem-solving negotiation and mediation.

11. A fifth evaluative criterion is procedural justice, which is perceived satisfaction with the fairness of a dispute resolution procedure. Research has shown that disputants prefer third-party procedures that provide opportunities for outcome control and voice. See Lind, E. A., and Tyler, T. R. *The Social Psychology of Procedural Justice.* New York: Plenum, 1988; Brett, J. M. "Commentary on Procedural Justice Papers." In R. J. Lewicki, B. H. Sheppard, and M. H. Bazer-

man (eds.), *Research on Negotiations in Organizations.* Greenwich, Conn.: JAI Press, 1986, 81–90.

We do not include procedural justice as a separate evaluation criterion for two reasons. First, unlike transaction costs, satisfaction with outcome, effect on the relationship, and recurrence, procedural justice is meaningful only at the level of a single procedure for a single dispute. It neither generalizes across the multiple procedures that may be used in the resolution of a single dispute nor generalizes across disputes to construct a systems-level cost. The other costs will do both. For example, it is possible to measure the disputants' satisfaction with the outcome of a dispute, regardless of how many different procedures were used to resolve that dispute. Likewise, it is possible to measure satisfaction with outcomes in a system that handles many disputes by asking many disputants about their feelings. Second, while procedural justice and distributive justice (satisfaction with fairness of outcomes) are distinct concepts, they are typically highly correlated. See Lind, E. A., and Tyler, T. R. *The Social Psychology of Procedural Justice.* New York: Plenum, 1988.

12. Williamson, O. E. "Transaction Cost Economics: The Governance of Contractual Relations." *Journal of Law and Economics,* 1979, *22,* 233–261; Brett, J. M., and Rognes, J. K. "Intergroup Relations in Organizations." In P. S. Goodman and Associates, *Designing Effective Work Groups.* San Francisco: Jossey-Bass, 1986, 202–236.

13. For a summary of the evidence of a relationship between procedural and distributive justice—that is, satisfaction with process and with outcome—see Lind, E. A., and Tyler, T. R. *The Social Psychology of Procedural Justice.* New York: Plenum, 1988. Lind and Tyler also summarize the evidence showing a relationship between voice and satisfaction with the process. For evidence of the effect of participation in shaping the ultimate resolution beyond simply being able to accept or reject a third party's advice, see Brett, J. M., and Shapiro, D. L. "Procedural Justice: A Test of Competing Theories and Implications for Managerial Decision Making," unpublished manuscript.

14. Lax, D. A., and Sebenius, J. K. *The Manager as Negotiator.* New York: Free Press, 1986.

15. The empirical research supporting this statement compares mediation to arbitration or adjudication. Claimants prefer mediation to arbitration in a variety of settings: labor-management (Brett, J. M., and Goldberg, S. B. "Grievance Mediation in the Coal Industry: A Field Experiment." *Industrial and Labor Relations Review,* 1983, *37,* 49–69), small claims disputes (McEwen, C. A., and Maiman, R. J. "Small Claims Mediation in Maine: An Empirical Assessment." *Maine Law Review,* 1981, *33,* 237–268), and divorce (Pearson, J. "An Evaluation of Alternatives to Court Adjudication." *Justice System Journal,* 1982, 7, 420–444).

16. Some commentators argue that court procedures are always preferable to a negotiated settlement when issues of public importance are involved in a dispute (see, for example, Fiss, O. M. "Against Settlement." *Yale Law Journal,* 1984, *93,* 1073–1090), and all agree that disputants should not be pressured into the settlement of such disputes. The extent to which parties should be encouraged to resolve disputes affecting a public interest is, however, not at all clear. See Edwards, H. T. "Alternative Dispute Resolution: Panacea or Anathema?" *Harvard Law Review,* 1986, *99,* 668–684.

Chapter Two

1. Goldberg, S. B., Green, E. D., and Sander, F.E.A. *Dispute Resolution.* Boston: Little, Brown, 1985, p. 548.

2. Davis, A. M. "Dispute Resolution at an Early Age." *Negotiation Journal,* 1986, *2,* 287–298.

3. Recorded conversation with Christopher Moore, May 18, 1987, pp. 60–61.

4. Dunlop, J. T. *Dispute Resolution, Negotiation, and Consensus Building.* Dover, Mass.: Auburn House, 1984, p. 157.

5. Davis, A. M. "Dispute Resolution at an Early Age." *Negotiation Journal,* 1986, *2,* 289.

6. Letter from Sylvia Skratek to authors, Oct. 14, 1987, p. 3.

7. McGovern, F. E. "Toward a Functional Approach for Managing Complex Litigation." *University of Chicago Law Review,* 1986, *53,* 440-493.

8. Ury, W. L. "Strengthening International Mediation." *Negotiation Journal,* 1987, *3,* 225-229.

9. Interview with Deborah Kolb, Oct. 23, 1987.

10. See Milhauser, M. "Corporate Culture and ADR." *Alternatives to the High Cost of Litigation,* 1988, *6,* 40-43.

Chapter Three

1. "The 'Wise Man' Procedure." *Alternatives to the High Cost of Litigation,* 1987, *5,* 105, 110-111.

2. Brock, J. *Bargaining Beyond Impasse.* Dover, Mass.: Auburn House, 1982.

3. Friedman, E. "Dispute Resolution in the Catholic Archdiocese of Chicago." Paper presented at the Dispute Resolution Research Colloquium, Northwestern University, Evanston, Ill., Jan. 13, 1988.

4. McKersie, R. B., and Shropshire, W. W. "Avoiding Written Grievances: A Successful Program." *Journal of Business,* 1962, *35,* 144.

5. Ibid., p. 146.

6. Bacow, L., and Mulkey, J. "Overcoming Local Opposition to Hazardous Waste Facilities: The Massachusetts Approach." *Harvard Environmental Law Review,* 1982, *6,* 265-305.

7. Susskind, L., and McMahon, G. "The Theory and Practice of Negotiated Rulemaking." *Yale Journal on Regulation,* 1985, *3,* 133-165.

8. Ibid., p. 137.

9. Ibid., pp. 160-163.

10. "CPR Legal Program Proceedings: VII. ADR Contract Clauses." *Alternatives to the High Cost of Litigation,* 1987, *5,* 101-103; quoting G. E. Moore, p. 101.

11. Rowe, M. P. "The Non-Union Complaint System at MIT: An Upward-Feedback Mediation Model." *Alternatives to the High Cost of Litigation,* 1984, *2,* 10-13.

12. Kochan, T. A., Katz, H. C., and McKersie, R. B. *The Transformation of American Industrial Relations.* New York: Basic Books, 1986, p. 95.

13. Ibid.

14. Goldberg, S. B., Green, E. D., and Sander, F.E.A. *Dispute Resolution.* Boston: Little, Brown, 1985, 283–284.

15. Susskind, L., and Cruikshank, J. *Breaking the Impasse: Consensual Approaches to Resolving Public Disputes.* New York: Basic Books, 1987, p. 145.

16. Davis, A. M. "Dispute Resolution at an Early Age." *Negotiation Journal,* 1986, *2,* 287–298.

17. Telephone interview with Karl Slaikeu, Mar. 25, 1988.

18. Whether court officers, judges, or others with power over disputants should use that power to encourage mediation is a matter of considerable debate. Some commentators view such conduct as inappropriate coercion. Others, accepting the element of coercion, argue that a bit of a push toward mediation does not seem too serious as long as the disputants are free to choose any outcome in the mediation. See Goldberg, S. B., Green, E. D., and Sander, F.E.A. *Dispute Resolution.* Boston: Little, Brown, 1985, p. 490.

19. Davis, A. M. "Dispute Resolution at an Early Age." *Negotiation Journal,* 1986, *2,* 289.

20. For a cautious but generally favorable perspective on the value of mediation in situations such as this, see Singer, L. R. "Nonjudicial Dispute Resolution Mechanisms: The Effects on Justice for the Poor." *Clearinghouse Review,* 1979, *13,* 569–583.

21. McGovern, F. E. "Toward a Functional Approach for Managing Complex Litigation." *University of Chicago Law Review,* 1986, *33,* 440–493.

22. Goldberg, S. B., Green, E. D., and Sander, F.E.A. *Dispute Resolution.* Boston: Little, Brown, 1985, pp. 225–243.

23. Ibid., pp. 271–280.

24. Ibid., pp. 282–283.

25. Dunlop, J. T. *Dispute Resolution, Negotiation, and Consensus Building.* Dover, Mass.: Auburn House, 1984, p. 157.

26. Ury, W. L. *Beyond the Hotline.* Boston: Houghton Mifflin, 1985.

27. Davis, A. M. "Dispute Resolution at an Early Age." *Negotiation Journal,* 1986, *2,* 287–298.

28. Goldberg, S. B., Green, E. D., and Sander, F.E.A. *Dispute Resolution.* Boston: Little, Brown, 1985, p. 189.

29. Ibid.

30. This really is using arbitration in its broadest sense. Managers determining the resolution of a dispute will often have no rights standard against which to judge the claims of the parties and may not provide any structured procedure for the presentation of evidence and arguments. Research on managers acting as third parties in dispute resolution indicates that managers may do a number of things: restructure the organization so that disputants do not have to come into contact; fire or transfer one or both; act as inquisitor-judges, doing their own investigation and making a decision; or throw resources at the problem. Kolb, D. M. "Who Are Organizational Third Parties and What Do They Do?" In R. J. Lewicki, B. H. Sheppard, and M. H. Bazerman (eds.), *Research on Negotiations in Organizations.* Greenwich, Conn.: JAI Press, 1986, 207–227; Kolb, D. M., and Sheppard, B. H. "Do Managers Mediate or Even Arbitrate?" *Negotiation Journal,* 1985, *1,* 379–388; Sheppard, B. H. "Managers as Inquisitors: Some Lessons from the Law." In M. H. Bazerman and R. J. Lewicki (eds.), *Negotiating in Organizations.* Newbury Park, Calif.: Sage, 1983.

31. But see McGillicuddy, N. B., Welton, G. L., and Pruitt, D. G. "Third-Party Intervention: A Field Experiment Comparing Three Different Models." *Journal of Personality and Social Psychology,* 1987, *53,* 104–112.

32. Goldberg, S. B., Green, E. D., and Sander, F.E.A. *Dispute Resolution.* Boston: Little, Brown, 1985, p. 282.

33. McGillis, D. *Consumer Dispute Resolution: A Survey of Programs.* Washington, D.C.: National Institute for Dispute Resolution, 1987.

34. Known as a "nonstoppage" strike, this procedure is discussed in Dunlop, J. T. *Dispute Resolution, Negotiation,*

and Consensus Building. Dover, Mass.: Auburn House, 1984, p. 165; Raiffa, H., and Lax, D. A. "Touchdowns in the Football Impasse." *Los Angeles Times,* Nov. 9, 1987, p. 7.

35. Katz, N., and Uhler, K. L. "An Alternative to Violence: Nonviolent Struggle for Change." In A. Goldstein (ed.), *Prevention and Control of Aggression,* New York: Pergamon, 1983.

36. Allison, G. "Rule of Prudence." In G. Allison and W. Ury (eds.), *Windows of Opportunity: Toward Peaceful Competition in U.S.-Soviet Relations,* forthcoming.

37. Rowe, M. P. "The Non-Union Complaint System at MIT: An Upward-Feedback Mediation Model." *Alternatives to the High Cost of Litigation,* 1984, *2,* 10–13.

38. McGillis, D. *Consumer Dispute Resolution: A Survey of Programs.* Washington, D.C.: National Institute for Dispute Resolution, 1985, pp. 13–14.

39. For an interesting discussion of forums, see Dunlop, J. T., and Salter, M. S. "Note on Forums and Governance." Harvard Business School Working Paper 0-388-046, 1987.

40. Kanter, R. M., and Morgan, E. "The New Alliances: First Report on the Formation and Significance of a Labor-Management 'Business Partnership.'" Harvard Business School Working Paper, 87-042, 1987.

Chapter Four

1. Recorded conversation with Richard A. Salem, May 14, 1987, p. 13.

2. Goldberg, S. B., Green, E. D., and Sander, F.E.A. *Dispute Resolution.* Boston: Little, Brown, 1985, pp. 225–232, 284–285.

3. Ibid., p. 540.

4. Ibid., pp. 541–543.

5. Graybeal, S. "Negotiating an Accident Prevention Center: The Experience of the Standing Consultative Commission." In J. W. Lewis and C. D. Blacker (eds.), *Next Steps to the Creation of an Accidental Nuclear War Prevention*

Center. Stanford, Calif.: Center for International Security and Arms Control, 1983, pp. 25–38.

6. Survey feedback, an organizational change technique, might also be used to involve the parties in the diagnosis and design process. See Nadler, D. "The Use of Feedback for Organizational Change: Promises and Pitfalls." *Group and Organizational Studies,* 1976, *1,* 177–186, for a description of this technique, and Peck, D. L., and Hollub, R. H. "Conflict, Intervention, and Resolution: The Third Party's Negotiated Role." *Evaluation and Program Planning,* forthcoming, for an example of the procedure in use. In applying survey feedback to the design of dispute resolution systems, the designer might ask a broad cross section of people involved in the system to participate in developing questions about the way disputes are resolved and then administer a survey containing these questions. The designer would summarize the results and hold a series of feedback meetings in which people involved in the dispute resolution system would interpret the results and begin to develop an agenda for change. For their technique of managing such a meeting, see also Blake, R. R., Sheppard, H. A., and Mouton, J. S. *Managing Intergroup Conflict in Industry.* Houston, Tex.; Gulf, 1964, and Blake, R. R., and Mouton, J. S. *Solving Costly Organizational Conflicts: Achieving Intergroup Trust, Cooperation, and Teamwork.* San Francisco: Jossey-Bass, 1984.

7. Recorded conversation with Susan Wildau, May 18, 1987, p. 31.

8. Recorded conversation with Christopher Moore, May 18, 1987, pp. 33–34.

9. Alderfer, C. P. "Organization Development." *Annual Review of Psychology,* 1977, *28,* pp. 197–223; Mirvis, P. H., and Berg, D. N. (eds.). *Failures in Organization Development and Change: Cases and Essays for Learning.* New York: Wiley, 1977, p. 53.

10. Fisher, R., and Ury, W. L. *Getting to Yes.* Boston: Houghton Mifflin, 1981, pp. 118–122.

11. The concept underlying the multidoor courthouse is that different types of disputes are amenable to different

dispute resolution procedures. Instead of just one "door" leading to the courtroom, such a center would have many doors through which individuals might pass to get to the most appropriate "room." Among the doors might be ones labeled "arbitration," "mediation," and "ombudsman." Goldberg, S. B., Green, E. D., and Sander, F.E.A. *Dispute Resolution.* Boston: Little, Brown, 1985, p. 514.

12. Edelman, P. B. "Institutionalizing Dispute Resolution Alternatives." *Justice System Journal*, 1984, *9*, 134–150.

13. Our failure to deal directly with miners at Caney Creek caused us to misperceive the strength of their distrust of management, with potentially disastrous results. Other union-management intervenors have also suffered from their lack of contact with employees. See Lewicki, R. J., and Alderfer, C. P. "The Tensions Between Research and Intervention in Intergroup Conflict." *Journal of Applied Behavioral Science*, 1973, *9*, 423–468.

14. Recorded conversation with Michael Lewis, May 14, 1987, pp. 24 and 46.

15. See Staw, B. M. "The Experimenting Organization: Problems and Prospects." In B. M. Staw, (ed.), *Psychological Foundations of Organizational Behavior.* Santa Monica, Calif.: Goodyear, 1977, pp. 466–486.

16. Recorded conversation with Raymond Shonholtz, May 12, 1987, p. 34.

17. Recorded conversation with Christopher Moore, May 18, 1987, p. 81. Scorable games have also been used to simulate forthcoming negotiations and to teach the parties to negotiate. See McGovern, F. E. "Toward a Functional Approach for Managing Complex Litigation." *University of Chicago Law Review*, 1986, *53*, 440–493.

18. Recorded conversation with Linda Singer, May 14, 1987, p. 22.

19. Riskin, L. L. "Mediation and Lawyers." *Ohio State University Law Journal*, 1982, *43*, 29–60.

20. Locke, E. A., Shaw, K. N., Saari, L. M., and Latham, G. P. "Goal Setting and Task Performance: 1969–1980." *Psychological Bulletin*, 1981, *90*, 125–152.

21. McKersie, R. B., and Shropshire, W. W. "Avoiding Written Grievances: A Successful Program." *Journal of Business*, 1962, *35*, 144.

22. McKersie, R. B. "Avoiding Written Grievances by Problem-Solving: An Outside View." *Personnel Psychology*, 1964, *17*, 377.

23. Wexley, K. N., and Latham, G. P. *Developing and Training Human Resources in Organizations.* Glenview, Ill.: Scott, Foresman, 1981.

24. Davis, A. M. "Dispute Resolution at an Early Age." *Negotiation Journal*, 1986, *2*, 287–298.

25. Recorded conversation with Michael Lewis, May 14, 1987, pp. 40–41.

26. Recorded conversation with Christopher Moore, May 18, 1987, p. 80; letter from Karl Slaikeu to authors, Nov. 5, 1987. See also Slaikeu, K. A., and MacDonald, C. B. *Conflict Resolution in Churches: A Model for Systems Consultation.* Austin, Tex.: Center for Conflict Management, 1987.

27. The theory and practice of program evaluation constitute an entire field of study that we can but touch on here.

28. Walton, R. "The Diffusion of New Work Structures: Explaining Why Success Didn't Take." In P. H. Mirvis and D. N. Berg (eds.), *Failures in Organization Development and Change.* New York: Wiley, 1977, pp. 243–263.

29. Goldberg, S. B., Green, E. D., and Sander, F.E.A. *Dispute Resolution.* Boston: Little, Brown, 1985, pp. 226, 372.

Chapter Five

1. A wildcat strike is a work stoppage during the term of a collective bargaining contract that is not authorized by that contract.

2. Because of the solidarity within the miners' union, the appearance of a single picket, frequently hooded to avoid recognition by management, would nearly always result in a sympathy strike.

3. The federal judge was acting to enforce the collective bargaining agreement between the United Mine Workers

of America (UMWA) and the Bituminous Coal Operators Association, which contains an implicit prohibition of strikes over arbitrable issues.

4. Data from the files of the Bituminous Coal Operators' Association.

5. Getman, J. G., Goldberg, S. B., and Herman, J. B. *Union Representation Elections: Law and Reality.* New York: Sage, 1976.

6. Our access to these officials was largely a result of Goldberg's reputation as an arbitrator in the coal industry. In the prior three years, he had arbitrated approximately 250 cases.

7. Kerr, C., and Siegal, A. "The Interindustry Propensity to Strike—An International Comparison." In A. W. Kornhauser, R. Dubin, and A. M. Ross (eds.), *Industrial Conflict.* New York: McGraw-Hill, 1954.

8. Dix, K., Fuller, C., Linsky, J., and Robinson, C. *Work Stoppages in the Appalachian Bituminous Coal Industry.* Morgantown, W.V.: Institute for Labor Studies, 1972.

9. In order to investigate this question, it was necessary to partition wildcat strikes into three categories: local strikes, sympathy strikes, and strikes motivated by political or national union issues. Local strikes were limited to a single mine site. Sympathy strikes occurred when a picket from one mine appeared at another. Miners were also using wildcat strikes as a political weapon. In 1975, for example, roving bands of pickets shut down most of the mines in West Virginia in protest of the state legislature's proposed changes in school textbooks. Widespread strikes in 1976 protested a nationwide change in the miners' health and welfare policy. Only the data on local strikes were used for this study.

10. The BCOA records we had been given proved inadequate. Their reliability was poor, and they did not contain information about mines where no strikes had occurred. We turned instead to those companies that had signed the UMWA contract, asking them to identify the mines they operated and provide the following information for each mine: its strike record for 1975 and 1976, the number of miners employed, the

coal extraction process, the location of the mine, the type of mining (surface or underground), its productivity, its injury rate, and its policy for dealing with wildcat strikes. For a more extensive description of our methods, see Brett, J. M., and Goldberg, S. B. "Wildcat Strikes in Bituminous Coal Mining." *Industrial and Labor Relations Review*, 1979, *32*, 465–483.

11. James Medoff, who had analyzed industry-level data and concluded that productivity was low at high-strike mines, reanalyzed our data in 1980 using more sophisticated methods than we had used. He, too, found no correlation between productivity and wildcat strikes in our data.

12. We chose District 17 in West Virginia for two reasons. First, it was the district with the third-highest strike frequency, averaging 3.9 strikes per mine in 1975 and 1976. Second, we thought that we could get cooperation for the study in that district. Goldberg had arbitrated there frequently and had good relations with the district leadership and with the labor relations representatives of several companies. To arrange for cooperation, Goldberg met with District 17 president Jack Perry and officials of each company. He met with the mine committee at each of the four mines along with the union representative servicing these mines.

13. We used a variety of devices to demonstrate the legitimacy of the study and maximize cooperation. Besides the meetings with the mine committees, we sent each miner a letter describing the study, as well as a copy of the letter we had received from UMWA president Arnold Miller. These efforts paid off, as only 2 of 124 miners refused to participate.

14. The Arbitration Review Board, which functioned in the coal industry from 1974 through 1979, reviewed approximately 10 percent of all arbitration decisions.

15. The UMWA constitution in effect at that time prohibited miners from engaging in strikes not authorized by the union and provided for a fine of up to $200 for violations of the prohibition.

16. Walton, R. *Interpersonal Peacemaking: Confrontations and Third-Party Consultation*. Reading, Mass.: Addison-Wesley, 1969.

17. Blake, R. R., Sheppard, H. A., and Mouton, J. S. *Managing Intergroup Conflict in Industry.* Houston, Tex.: Gulf, 1964.

18. Campbell, J. P., and Dunnette, M. D. "Effectiveness of T-Group Experiences in Managerial Training and Development." *Psychological Bulletin,* 1968, *70,* 73–104.

19. The literature on attitude change shows clearly that attitudes will change subsequent to a change in behavior. McGuire, W. J. "The Nature of Attitudes and Attitude Change." In G. Lindzey and E. Aronson (eds.), *Handbook of Social Psychology.* Reading, Mass.: Addison-Wesley, 1969, *3,* pp. 136–314.

20. The current UMWA constitution provides that only the international president can authorize a strike but contains no provision for sanctions on union members who strike without authorization. UMWA Constitution, 1983, Article 19, Section 7.

21. The President's Commission on Coal. Labor-Management Seminar III, "Factors Affecting Wildcat Strikes." Washington, D.C.: U.S. Government Printing Office, 1979, pp. 1–9, 70–74.

Chapter Six

1. The names Williams and Sexton are pseudonyms, as are all the names we use for union and management officials associated with Caney Creek.

2. As discussed earlier, the contractual grievance procedure has four steps. In step 1, the miner talks to his foreman. In step 2, the mine committee and a senior management official become involved in the negotiation. In step 3, a union district representative enters the negotiation for one last try at settlement. Step 4 is arbitration.

3. Under the contract between the miners and the operators, a job that is not filled by a qualified applicant from the mine work force or a laid-off miner may be awarded to a new employee.

4. Schein, E. H. *Organizational Psychology.* (3rd ed.) Englewood Cliffs, N.J.: Prentice-Hall, 1980, pp. 22–24.

5. The President's Commission on Coal. Labor-Management Seminar III, "Factors Affecting Wildcat Strikes." Washington, D.C.: U.S. Government Printing Office, 1979, p. 63.

6. Kolb, D. M. "Who Are Organizational Third Parties and What Do They Do?" In R. J. Lewicki, B. H. Sheppard, and M. H. Bazerman (eds.), *Research on Negotiations in Organizations*. Greenwich, Conn.: JAI Press, 1986.

7. Telephone conversation with authors, Feb. 15, 1988.

8. Ibid.

9. Telephone conversation with authors, Mar. 3, 1988.

Chapter Seven

1. Idle day work must be equally shared in accordance with past practice and custom. National Bituminous Coal Wage Agreement of 1971, Article IV, Section (c) (7).

2. Brett, J. M., and Goldberg, S. B. "Wildcat Strikes in Bituminous Coal Mining." *Industrial and Labor Relations Review*, 1979, *32*, 465–483.

3. While it is the practice to refer to the contractual grievance "procedure," and while we follow that practice, it should be clear that what is involved is not one procedure, but two: a three-step negotiation procedure followed by an arbitration procedure.

4. *Vaca* v. *Sipes*, 386 U.S. 171 (1967).

5. Fleming, R. W. *The Labor Arbitration Process.* Urbana: University of Illinois Press, 1967.

6. Goldberg, S. B. "The Mediation of Grievances Under a Collective Bargaining Contract: An Alternative to Arbitration." *Northwestern University Law Review*, 1982, *77*, 270–315. These figures should not be taken as indicating widespread use of grievance mediation. As of 1979, only 3 percent of all U.S. collective bargaining contracts provided for grievance mediation, and the procedure was rarely used. Indeed, except for occasional journal articles suggesting a greater use of grievance mediation, the procedure was essentially unknown in U.S. labor relations in the early 1980s.

7. Goldberg, S. B., and Hobgood, W. P. *Mediating Grievances: A Cooperative Solution.* Washington, D.C.: Bureau of Labor-Management Relations and Cooperative Programs, U.S. Department of Labor, 1987.

8. For other arguments for and against the use of med-arb, see Chapter Three. The desire to preserve the mediation aspect of our proposed intervention also led us to reject the expedited arbitration procedure that some industries use in an effort to reduce the cost and expense of conventional arbitration. Whatever the value of expedited arbitration in those respects, it is at best low-cost adjudication rather than an aid to interests-based negotiation.

9. The availability of mediation was also unattractive to some arbitrators, who feared that mediation threatened to reduce the demand for arbitrators. While arbitral opposition would not of itself prevent an employer and union from experimenting with mediation, the unfavorable opinion of a respected arbitrator might influence their decision. We sought to deal with this source of potential opposition by encouraging arbitrators with an interest in mediation to learn and play the mediator's role.

10. Beginning in April, 1981, the costs of arbitration were borne entirely by the participating companies and union districts.

11. Valtin, R. "Discussion: Mediation of Grievances." *Proceedings,* 35th Annual Meeting, Industrial Relations Research Association. Madison, Wis.: Industrial Relations Research Association, 1983, pp. 260–264.

12. Warren, J. "Mediation Cools Off the Coalfields." *Chicago Tribune,* Oct. 8, 1985, Sec. 3, p. 1. Copyright © Chicago Tribune Company, all rights reserved, used with permission.

13. After each case, the mediator submitted to us a form that reported whether a settlement was reached and, if so, the terms of the settlement. These forms, which also reported the mediator's fees for that case, were subsequently used as a basis for our annual report to the parties.

14. We do not have the details of the remaining 27 per-

cent of the settlements, as they took place after the mediation had concluded.

15. See also Sarno, F. "A Management Approach." *Proceedings*, 36th Annual Meeting, National Academy of Arbitrators. Washington, D.C.: Bureau of National Affairs, 1984, pp. 136–139. (Third-step settlement rate increased significantly in Indiana and remained virtually the same in Illinois.)

16. The arbitration average is not industrywide but is limited to District 28, where more mediation has taken place than in any other district.

17. If we had had the opportunity, we would have argued that the mediator has no power to interfere with the operations of the company; only company representatives who enter into unsound agreements in mediation can do that. The arbitrator, in contrast, does have the power to issue binding decisions without the consent of company representatives, and without regard for the effect of the decision on company operations.

18. One coal company and another company in a different industry have ceased mediating for this reason. Thus, it would appear that one limitation on mediation is that if either party is subject to pressures that make reasonable compromises difficult, the procedure cannot succeed. On the company side, such pressure might come from operating personnel with the power to direct the activities of the labor relations personnel who represent the company in mediation. We are aware of one company where that power has been used regularly to frustrate agreements that appeared to meet the interests of both parties. We doubt that the union will be willing to mediate with that company much longer.

19. The MREP board of directors consists of Brett, Goldberg, William Hobgood, and Rolf Valtin. The MREP Administrative Services Office has been under the capable supervision of Dawn Harris since it opened in 1983.

20. To some extent, the heavy reliance on arbitration in the railroad industry is because the U.S. government, not the parties, pays the arbitrator's fees and expenses. See Nolan, D. R., and Abrams, R. I. "American Labor Arbitration: The Early Years." *University of Florida Law Review*, 1983, *35*, 373–421.

21. Goldberg, S. B. "The Mediation of Grievances Under a Collective Bargaining Contract: An Alternative to Arbitration." *Northwestern University Law Review,* 1982, *77,* 270–315.

22. The tendency of lawyers to oppose the use of non-adjudicative modes of dispute resolution has been noted in contexts other than that of grievance mediation. Riskin, L. L. "Mediation and Lawyers." *Ohio State University Law Journal,* 1982, *43,* 29–60; Goldberg, S. B., Green, E. D., and Sander, F.E.A. *Dispute Resolution.* Boston: Little, Brown, 1985, pp. 486–488. In the coal industry, the collective bargaining contract prohibits the parties from being represented by lawyers in arbitration, so opposition by lawyers for economic reasons has not been a problem there.

23. The average cost of arbitration nationwide from 1983 to 1986 was $1,408, and the average time from the request for arbitration to the receipt of the arbitration award was 235 days. Federal Mediation and Conciliation Service. *39th Annual Report, Fiscal Year 1986.* Washington, D.C.: U.S. Government Printing Office, 1988.

Chapter Eight

1. See Goldman, R. M., *From Warriors to Politicians: Party Systems as Institutional Alternatives to Warfare.* Unpublished manuscript.

Index